For my beloved parents, George and Wilma Brockway,
who rest in the West Country

First published 2014
Mabecron Books
42 Drake Circus
Plymouth
PL4 8AB

Illustrations Rebecca Cobb
Designed by Peter Bennett

Typeset in Baskerville

10 9 8 7 6 5 4 3 2 1

ISBN 9780957256033

West Country Cakes
& Assorted
Fancies

Geraldene Holt

M
Mabecron Books

Guide to recipes

Unless stated otherwise: all cake tins are round; spoonfuls are level; butter is unsalted; sugar is caster; and eggs are large.

Baking instructions: are given for both conventional electric and gas ovens. Fan ovens may need to be turned to a lower setting on the thermostat allowing a reduction of approximately 10° per 100° so that 180°C is the equivalent of 200°C in a non-fan oven. An oven thermometer placed on the same shelf as the cake tin reveals the actual baking temperature of the cake.

Abbreviations: teaspoon - tsp; dessertspoon - dsp; tablespoon - tbs; gram - g; kilogram - kg; millilitre - ml; litre - l; millimetre - mm; centimetre - cm; metre - m; ounce - oz; pound - lb; fluid ounce - fl oz; pint – pt; inch - in.; foot - ft

Introduction

Is it, I wonder, simply childhood recollection that prompts me to make Lardy Cake now and again, even today when I no longer keep pigs or live in a pork-rearing region, and rarely bake with lard anyway? Home-made cakes appear to be particularly evocative, and perhaps it's not just their flavour that awakens our remembrance of time past but the warm memory of other people and earlier happy occasions; because cakes are a food that is best shared for the deepest enjoyment. Our national fondness for the food of the past still shapes much of what we eat in daily life, giving us a valuable sense of continuity that in a busy world we often scarcely notice or acknowledge ...yet which remains a precious legacy all the same.

The invitation to write this book about my favourite region was irresistible. I was exhilarated to revisit the domestic cooking found in cottages and farmhouses of the West Country. It was here that I rediscovered family recipes that depend on the characteristic ingredients of the area, some home-grown, others introduced as the result of its trading past: saffron and treacle, dried fruit and almonds, cinnamon and ginger, apples and cider, world-class butter and cream. These are the prime flavours of West Country cakes and I am delighted to share them with you.

For the last thirty years the West Country has been described as the California of Britain and in the same way that the West Coast region of the United States has attracted people of vision and enterprise, our south-westerly peninsular has been a magnet for initiative. As I travelled around these four counties that share one continuous coastline, I was inspired anew by the variety and diversity of West Country food production. Each county has working flour mills, produces apple cider and makes superlative ice cream, yet each maintains its own character and identity.

Farmers and growers know how to get the best from their land and many have diversified to produce speciality foods, with hundreds of small artisan enterprises producing high-quality ingredients, food and drink. Each county has continued to produce its most celebrated foods: Dorset Knobs, Somerset cider and perry, Devonshire honey, and Cornish clotted cream, but nowadays Cornwall also produces home-grown tea, Devon has a chocolatier, Somerset is known for its well-aged apple brandy, and Dorset provides the nation with fresh juicy blueberries.

This book is a personal collection of recipes drawing on the flavours and ingredients of the West Country. It includes a variety of traditional delights: Cornish Splits and Saffron cake, Devonshire Revel buns and Cider cake, Dorset Matrimony cake and Custard tarts, along with Sedgemoor Easter cake and Bath Buns from Somerset. Then there are some of the most popular cakes that I baked for two decades in my own Devon kitchen, such as Harvest Fruit cake, Otterton gingerbread, Lime Curd tarts and a Chocolate Ice Cream Blizzard cake. To these I've added many of my latest cakes inspired by the finest produce of the West Country, such as Hot Strawberry tarts, Elderflower and Almond Meringue cake, Apricot Trifle cake, little Walnut and Honey cakes and Triple Ice Cream Marble cake. I hope you find enjoyment in these pages - a celebration of this unique region of Britain.

Cornwall, pages 12-39
Wholemeal Oat Scones ♦ Bramble Jelly ♦
Saffron Cake ♦ Treacle Loaf ♦ Cornish
Potato Cakes ♦ Butterscotch Curls ♦ Heavva
or Heavy Cake ♦ Cornish Black Cake ♦
Raspberry and Almond Cake ♦ Chocolate
Tipsy Cake ♦ Chestnut Sponge Cake ♦
Brandy Snap Baskets with Cornish Tea Ice
Cream ♦ Cornish Tea Ice Cream ♦ Rose
Geranium Leaf Cake ♦ Autumn Harvest
Crumble Cake ♦ Figgy Hobbin ♦ Honey and
Walnut Cakes ♦ Congress Tarts ♦ Triple Ice
Cream Marble Cake ♦ Hot Blackberry Cake ♦
Easter Biscuits ♦

Devonshire, pages 48-81
Devonshire Fruit Loaf ♦ Sidmouth
Wholemeal Scones ♦ Braunton Revel Buns ♦
Beekeeper's Honey Cake ♦ Cider Cake ♦
Chocolate Cake filled with Devon Cream ♦
Wholewheat Sponge Cake with Fudge Filling ♦
Orange Sponge Cake with Citrus Curd ♦
Chocolate Cranberry Cake with Yoghurt Frosting ♦
Clyst William Barton Cake ♦ Otterton Mill
Gingerbread ♦ Rose Petal Sponge Cake with
Rose Petal Cream ♦ Honiton Cattern Cakes ♦
Lime Curd Tarts ♦ Chocolate Coconut Squares
Hot Strawberry Tarts ♦ Devon Blizzard Cake ♦
Apple Sauce Cake ♦ Plymtree Harvest Cake ♦
Devon Apple Butter ♦

West Country Cream Tea, pages 40-47
Cornish Clotted Cream ♦ Fresh Strawberry
Jam ♦ Cake Stall Plain Scones ♦ Cornish
Splits & Devonshire Chudleighs ♦

Somerset, pages 82-115
Sally Lunn Teacakes ♦ Apple and Cheddar
Cheese Scone Ring ♦ Bath Buns ♦ Somerset
Raisin Glory ♦ Sedgemoor Easter Cake ♦
Spiced Apple Cake with Apple Brandy
Cream ♦ Ripe Raspberry Roll ♦ Lavender and
Orange Cake ♦ Cider Fruit Cake ♦ Pear and
Perry Cake ♦ Frosted Yoghurt Cake ♦
Somerset Mincemeat Pies ♦ Somerset
Mincemeat ♦ Toffee Apples ♦ Gingerbread
Valentines ♦ Japonais Cakes ♦ Eleventh Hour
Kisses ♦ Walnut Meringues filled with Coffee
Cream ♦ Digestive Biscuits ♦ Dark Chocolate
Brandy Mousse Cake ♦ Boiled Fruit Cake ♦
Bath Teashop Brownies ♦

Dorset, pages 116-152
Fruit and Nut Buttermilk Bread ♦ Wholemeal
Fruit Scones ♦ Hazelnut, Cranberry and
Banana Loaf ♦ Cann Mills Hot Cross Buns ♦
Lardy Cake ♦ Spiced Carrot Cake ♦
Caraway Seed Cake ♦ Matrimony Cake ♦
Elderflower and Almond Meringue Cake ♦
Chocolate Fondant Cake with Raspberries and
Cream ♦ Walnut Shortcake topped with Blueberry
Meringue ♦ Upside-down Orange Marmalade
and Pineapple Cake ♦ West Country Syllabub ♦
Almond Tuiles with Syllabub ♦ Custard Tarts ♦
Lemon Pies ♦ Lemon Curd ♦ Dorset Fluffy
Cakes with Orange Flower Water ♦
Dorset Apple Cake ♦ Apricot Trifle Cake ♦
Rosemary and Lavender Shortbread Biscuits ♦
Ginger Fairings ♦ Dorset Chocolate Truffles ♦

Cornwall

I remember running quickly across the stubble field with my brothers, jumping over the wheat stalks that scratched our ankles; over the stile and down the lane, past the village baker with the enticing aroma of freshly-baked bread and hot pasties drifting out of the shop. We would arrive, breathless with anticipation, at Auntie Lily's open kitchen door and sit at the table, gazing at the huge American refrigerator in the corner. We knew it held that most prized of foods - homemade ice cream! Rich, buttercup-yellow, with clotted cream, it was a dream come true. Ice cream was so rarely available in post-war, ration-book Britain, so this particular childhood memory is truly unforgettable.

We would travel from London on the legendary Cornish Riviera Express and I remember longing for that captivating moment while crossing Brunel's Royal Albert Bridge, over the river Tamar, when the sweeping curve would allow us to glimpse both the engine and guard's van of our train. Every Cornish holiday revealed more edible delights: saffron buns and heavy cake; warm splits laden with clotted cream and black treacle; bowls of fragrant strawberries; and cherries picked from the tree. It's small wonder that I've always seen Cornwall as a land of plenty.

Historically the industrial revolution brought wealth to Cornwall and the arrival of the railway a way of distributing its food produce to markets across the country. The classic wooden strawberry punnet was invented in the Tamar valley as a durable, breathable, damage proof container for rail transportation of the delicate and delicious early strawberries. As the mining industry waned Cornwall looked to the future by drawing on its past centuries of food production. Fresh locally grown ingredients and specialities such as the famed clotted cream are particularly identified with Cornwall; produce which still provides the mainstay of the county's diet and which can be found throughout its long baking history.

Recent trends have been surprising. Who would have thought that Cornwall could produce its own whiskey? Yet David Healey, the founder of a cyder farm, was persuaded, by his head brewer Roger Ryman, to try. Hicks & Healey's Cornish Single Malt 7-year-old whiskey is now a going concern, and highly-rated by many. Perhaps more astonishing is that Cornwall is now growing and harvesting tea, even exporting packets of the prized leaves to Japan and China, the original home of the tea plant, Camellia Sinensis. The Tregothnan Estate, not far from Truro, has planted 25 acres with cuttings and seeds of tea plants from Darjeeling in India where the growing conditions are similar. This enterprising idea came from Tregothnan's head gardener, Jonathon Jones and his employers, the Boscawen family. Displaying the patience of true gardeners - because a tea plant takes seven years to mature - they are now rewarded with an annual harvest of 10 tons of tea leaves, sold at a premium price to dedicated connoisseurs.

Every year Cornwall's quality food is displayed at county shows, food festivals, and farmer's markets. It is also found in local shops and street stalls. On offer is superb produce: ice cream, yoghurt and cheese, a huge variety of fruit and vegetables, locally grown and milled grains, honey and herbs. This abundance of quality and variety has ensured that Cornwall's national reputation now lies not only with its distinguished writers, poets and painters but with its food producers and growers.

Recipes for Cornwall

16 Wholemeal Oat Scones
17 Bramble Jelly
18 Saffron Cake
20 Treacle Loaf
21 Cornish Potato Cakes
22 Butterscotch Curls
23 Heavva or Heavy Cake
24 Cornish Black Cake
25 Raspberry and Almond Cake
26 Chocolate Tipsy Cake
27 Chestnut Sponge Cake
28 Brandy Snap Baskets with Cornish Tea Ice Cream
29 Cornish Tea Ice Cream
30 Rose Geranium Leaf Cake
31 Autumn Harvest Crumble Cake
32 Figgy Hobbin
33 Honey and Walnut Cakes
34 Congress Tarts
36 Triple Ice Cream Marble Cake
38 Hot Blackberry Cake
39 Easter Biscuits

Wholemeal Oat Scones

An attractive scone with a crumbly texture and subtle, nutty flavour. Serve the scones warm with bramble jelly and clotted cream (p44).

Oven: 220°C/Fan 200°C/Gas 7 **Baking time:** 15 minutes **Makes:** about 20 scones
Equipment: 5cm fluted pastry cutter (optional); baking sheet, floured

175g (6oz) self-raising flour
2 teaspoons baking powder
1 teaspoon ground ginger
¼ teaspoon salt
175g (6oz) wholemeal plain flour
100g (3½oz) butter
60g (2oz) rolled oats
4 tablespoons honey
1 egg, whisked with milk to make 200ml (7fl oz)

Sift the flour, baking powder, ground ginger and salt into a mixing bowl. Stir in the wholemeal flour, add the butter in small pieces and rub in until the mixture resembles breadcrumbs then mix in the rolled oats. Blend the honey with the egg mixture and pour onto the dry ingredients. Mix together to make a soft sticky dough.

Turn onto a floured board and pat or roll until 1cm thick. Use either the pastry cutter to cut as many scones as possible or use a sharp knife to divide the dough into triangular pieces. Place the scones on the prepared baking sheet.

Bake in the preheated oven the scones are until well-risen and golden-brown. Cool the scones on the baking sheet for 2 minutes then serve straight away.

Bramble Jelly

The country name for the claret-coloured jelly made from ripe hedgerow blackberries which, depending on location, can be gathered from late summer to early autumn. Take care to collect blackberries before an early frost ruins the fruit - known as the devil's work in some parts of the West Country. Bramble jelly goes particularly well with freshly baked wholemeal scones.

2kg (4½lb) blackberries
2 lemons
500ml (1pt) water
sugar

Rinse the fruit in cold water and drain well. Tip the fruit into a preserving pan, add the juice of the lemons with the water and bring slowly to the boil. Simmer until the fruit is tender. Use a potato masher to crush the fruit and extract its purple juice and full flavour. Cool slightly then ladle the fruit and liquid into a muslin jelly bag or an old scalded pillowcase tied to a hook in the ceiling, or if need be, the legs of an upturned chair with a large bowl placed to catch the liquid. Leave overnight and resist the temptation to squeeze the bag which might make the jelly cloudy.

Next day, measure the blackberry liquid into the pan and for each 600ml (1pt) allow 450g (1lb) sugar. Stir over moderate heat until the sugar has dissolved then raise the heat and boil the mixture until setting point, 105°C, is reached. Remove from the heat, skim off any scum on the surface and ladle the jelly into small scalded jars. Seal tightly and leave the jars in place until the jelly is cold and has set. Then label and store in a cool, dark cupboard.

Saffron Cake

Bright, daffodil-yellow saffron with its bewitching scent and taste was once characteristic of much West Country baking - particularly in yeast-risen bread, buns and cakes. The plant originated in Western Asia and, by the sixteenth century, saffron was cultivated so successfully in Britain that Saffron Walden acquired its name. Nowadays the stigmas of Crocus Sativus are harvested by hand mainly in Spain and Iran, and are then dried to produce saffron's orange threads. Because it is the world's costliest spice, a cheaper food colouring is sometimes employed by commercial bakeries. Saffron survives today in Cornwall's Saffron Cake; when home-made, saffron's yellow liquid with its orange threads are mixed with flour, yeast, butter, sugar, currants and candied peel then baked in a loaf tin. To obtain the maximum colour and flavour from the spice, snip the saffron threads into short pieces before soaking overnight.

Oven: 180°C/Fan 160°C/Gas 4 **Baking time:** 45-60 minutes **Makes:** 12 portion cake
Equipment: 900g (2lb) loaf tin, lightly oiled

¼ teaspoon saffron
4 tablespoons boiling water
300g (10oz) white bread flour
1½ teaspoon rapid-rise dried yeast
60g (2oz) caster sugar
60g (2oz) butter or clotted cream
200ml (7fl oz) warm water
120g (4oz) currants
30g (1oz) candied peel, finely chopped

Glaze:
2 tablespoons milk
1 tablespoon sugar

Use scissors to cut the saffron threads into a teacup. Pour on the boiling water, stir well and leave overnight for the liquid to become deep yellow.

Mix together the flour, yeast and sugar then rub in the butter or add the cream with the saffron water including the threads. Stir in sufficient warm water to make a soft dough and beat until the dough feels elastic. Sprinkle the currants and candied peel on top of the dough and cover the bowl with roomy plastic bag then set aside in a warm place until doubled in size. Turn the dough on to a floured surface and gently knead for 1-2 minutes to distribute the dried fruit. Shape the dough into an oblong and place in the prepared loaf tin. Cover again and leave to rise. This will take some time, possibly 2-3 hours, while in a cold kitchen the dough can be left overnight.

Bake the cake in the preheated oven for 45 minutes or until the cake has a golden crust and is shrinking from the tin. Remove from the oven, turn the cake onto a wire rack and brush the top with the milk mixed with the sugar. Serve the cake slightly warm, cut into slices.

Treacle Loaf

Black treacle with its strong, caramel taste often figures in Cornish baking and, for many years, was cheaper than refined sugar. Considered a health-food containing the vitamin B6 by the nutritionist, Gaylord Hauser, who recommends a spoonful stirred into a mug of warm milk as a night-cap. In this recipe, the treacle contributes both colour and flavour to a fruity tea-bread which is sliced and eaten plain or spread with clotted cream.

Oven: 180°C/Fan 160°C/ Gas 4   **Baking time:** 1¼-1½ hours   **Makes:** 1 large/2 small loaves
Equipment: 1kg (2lb) loaf tin or two 500g (1lb) loaf tins, greased

350g (12oz) self-raising flour
120g (4oz) light muscovado sugar
¼ teaspoon mixed spice
½ teaspoon ground ginger
175g (6oz) sultanas
90g (3oz) candied peel, chopped
¼ teaspoon bicarbonate soda
4 tablespoons milk
175g (6oz) black treacle
1 egg, beaten

Sieve the flour, sugar and spices into a bowl and stir in the sultanas and candied peel. Blend the bicarbonate of soda with 1 tablespoon milk in a cup. Warm the rest of the milk in a pan with the treacle. Remove from the heat, add the bicarbonate of soda liquid and the beaten egg. Stir and pour onto the other ingredients in the mixing bowl. Mix until well combined and pour into the prepared tin(s).

Bake in the preheated oven for 30 minutes then lower the heat to 170°C/Fan 150°C/Gas 3 and bake for a further 45-60 minutes depending on size or until a slim bamboo skewer comes out clean from the centre. Cool the tea-bread in the tin(s) for 10 minutes then transfer to a wire rack.

Cornish Potato Cakes

From Scotland to Wales, and Cumbria to Cornwall, traditional potato-enriched bread, scones and cakes are either cooked on a griddle or baked in an oven. For centuries, Cornwall was famed for its fine potatoes, its mild climate often enabling a double crop to be cultivated. These baked potato cakes resemble fruit scones and are excellent served hot, either plain or split across and spread with butter or cream cheese.

Oven: 200°C/Fan 180°C/Gas 6 **Baking time:** 25-30 minutes **Makes:** 6-8 portions
Equipment: baking sheet, floured

230g (8oz) potatoes, boiled and peeled
230g (8oz) self-raising flour
120g (4oz) butter or suet, grated
30g (1oz) caster sugar
60g (2oz) currants
60g (2oz) candied orange peel, chopped
1 egg, beaten
4-5 tablespoons milk

Mash the potatoes into a bowl and add the flour, grated butter, sugar, currants and candied peel and stir well. Mix in the egg and enough milk to make a stiff dough. Shape into a ball and roll out until 2.5cm (1in.) thick circle or an oblong shape. Transfer the dough to the prepared baking sheet and use a sharp knife to mark 6-8 portions cutting half-way through.

Bake in the preheated oven until the potato cake is golden-brown. Cool on the tray for 5 minutes then transfer to a wooden board and cut through into separate portions.

Butterscotch Curls

Unusual spiced scones with spirals of butterscotch filling.

Oven: 200°C/Fan 180°C/Gas 7 **Baking time:** 20 minutes **Makes:** 12 scones
Equipment: 12 cup patty tin, buttered

230g (8oz) self-raising flour
1 teaspoon baking powder
¼ teaspoon ground cinnamon
120g (4oz) butter, softened
1 egg
125ml (4fl oz) milk
90g (3oz) light muscovado sugar

Sieve the flour, baking powder and cinnamon into a bowl. Add half the butter in pieces then rub in until mixture resembles breadcrumbs. Beat the egg with the milk and mix into the flour to make a soft dough. Shape the dough into a ball and roll out on a floured surface to an oblong 30 x 20cm.

Spread the remaining butter over the dough and sprinkle the sugar on top. Roll up the dough from the short side and cut into 12 slices. Place the slices, cut side up, in the prepared patty tin.

Bake in the preheated oven for 20 minutes. Transfer the scones to a wire rack and serve warm.

Heavva or Heavy Cake

The name of this famous flat cake, also known as Fuggan, is said to derive from the shout of 'Heave' as Cornish fishermen dragged their nets ashore. Early recipes specify lard and currants, this later, richer version contains butter and also candied peel. Sugar-crusted and marked with the pattern of a fishing net, this regional cake is still home-made and is also produced by local bakers.

Oven: 180°C/Fan 160°C/Gas 4 **Baking time:** 30-40 minutes **Makes:** 8 portion cake
Equipment: baking sheet, lightly buttered

230g (8oz) flour
60g (2oz) caster sugar
150g (5oz) butter
120g (4oz) currants
60g (2oz) candied peel, chopped
1 tablespoon milk
1 tablespoon granulated sugar

Sift the flour and sugar into a mixing bowl, add half the butter cut into pieces then rub in until the mixture resembles breadcrumbs. Stir in the currants and candied peel and mix to a stiff dough with 4-6 tablespoons cold water.

Roll out the dough to an oblong about 30 x 15cm (12 x 6in.) Dot the surface with small pieces of the remaining butter and fold over. Gently roll the dough to make a circle about 2.5cm (1in.) thick. Transfer the dough to the prepared baking sheet and brush with milk. Sprinkle with granulated sugar and use a sharp knife to mark a trellis pattern to resemble a fishing net.

Bake in the preheated oven until the cake is cooked and is turning golden at the edge. Cool on the baking sheet for 5 minutes then cut into portions and serve.

Cornish Black Cake

Dark with dried fruit and black treacle, this fine cake with a buttery flavour of spice and caramel is well suited to celebrations such as a birthday, anniversary or Christmas. A similar version appears across the river Tamar in Devon.

Oven: 160°C/Fan 140°C/Gas 3 **Baking time:** 2-2½ hours **Makes:** 1.8kg (4lb) cake
Equipment: 20cm (8in.) round or square lined cake tin

200g (7oz) butter
200g (7oz) dark muscovado sugar
120g (4oz) black treacle
4 eggs
350g (10 oz) plain flour
1 teaspoon baking powder
½ teaspoon ground cinnamon
¼ teaspoon grated nutmeg
500g (1lb 2oz) mixed seedless raisins, sultanas and currants
120g (4oz) chopped candied peel
100g (3½oz) blanched almonds, slivered

Cream the butter with the sugar until fluffy. Mix in the treacle and eggs, one at a time, with a little of the flour. Stir in the rest of the flour (sifted with the baking powder and spices), and the dried fruit, candied peel and almonds. The mixture should be quite stiff. Spoon into the prepared tin and smooth level.

Bake in the centre of a preheated oven until a slim bamboo skewer comes out clean from the centre. Cool the cake in the tin for 1 hour then turn onto a wire rack.

Raspberry and Almond Cake

A light, almond cake is baked with a layer of fresh raspberries and flaked almonds covering the top. Serve the cake warm with thick cream or ice cream.

Oven: 180°C/Fan 160°C/Gas 4 **Baking time:** 30-40 minutes **Makes:** 8 portion cake
Equipment: 20cm (8in.) spring-clip tin, buttered and base-lined

Cake Layer:
120g (4oz) butter
120g (4oz) caster sugar
2 eggs
few drops of almond essence or orange flower water
100g (3½oz) self-raising flour
60g (2oz) ground almonds

Fruit Layer:
300g (10 oz) ripe raspberries
15g (½oz) flaked almonds
1 tablespoon icing sugar

Cream the butter with the sugar until pale and fluffy. Beat in the eggs, one at a time. Stir in the essence and fold in the flour and ground almonds.

Spoon the mixture into the prepared cake tin and smooth level. Scatter half the flaked almonds over the mixture. Toss the raspberries with the rest of the almonds and the icing sugar and spoon over the cake in an even layer.

Bake in the preheated oven until a slim bamboo skewer comes out clean from the centre. Cool in the tin for 3 minutes then open the clip and remove the side. Serve the cake hot or warm.

Chocolate Tipsy Cake

In the eighteenth century, Tipsy Cake was another name for Brandy Trifle, and Eliza Acton states that 'the old-fashioned mode of preparing this dish was to soak a light sponge or Savoy cake in as much good French brandy as it could absorb'. For a traditional Tipsy Cake, use a plain sponge cake instead of the chocolate version here.

Oven: 190°C/Fan 170°C/Gas 5 **Baking time:** 40-45 minutes **Makes:** 10-12 portion cake
Equipment: 18-20cm (7-8in.) ring tin or 20cm (8in.) spring-clip tin, buttered

120g (4oz) caster sugar
120g (4oz) butter
2 eggs
3 tablespoons cocoa powder
3 tablespoons strong black coffee
100g (3½oz) self-raising flour
for decoration:
100-150ml (3½ - 5fl oz) French brandy or dark rum
150ml (5fl oz) double cream
1 egg white
1 tablespoon caster sugar
30g (1oz) chocolate curls or flakes (optional)

Tip a spoonful of the caster sugar into the buttered cake tin and tilt until lightly dusted with sugar. Return any surplus to the rest of the sugar in a bowl. Add the butter and beat until light and fluffy. Beat in the eggs alternately with the cocoa blended with the coffee. Fold in the sieved flour. Spoon the mixture into the prepared cake tin and smooth level.

Bake in the preheated oven for 30-35 minutes or until the cake is springy in the centre and just starting to shrink from the tin. Cool in the tin for 2 minutes then turn on to a wire rack.

When the cake is cold, place upside down on a flat plate with a slight rim to catch any surplus liquid. Slowly spoon over the brandy so that the cake absorbs it gradually. Beat the cream until thick but still glossy. In a separate bowl whisk the egg white until stiff, whisk in the sugar and then fold into the cream. Spread the cream over the cake in a thick layer leaving a rough finish. Decorate if you wish with curls of chocolate and set aside in a cool place for 1-2 hours before serving.

Chestnut Sponge Cake

Sweet chestnut trees grew in Cornwall three hundred years ago so maybe some of their progeny still flourish. I devised this light and appealing chestnut cake - which contains no wheat flour - as a contrast to the usual more solid variety.

Oven: 180°C/Fan 160°C/Gas 4 **Baking time:** 30-40 minutes **Makes:** 10-12 portion cake
Equipment: 23cm (9in.) spring-clip tin, buttered and base-lined

525g (1lb 4oz) sweet chestnut puree
1 teaspoon vanilla essence
5 eggs, separated
60g (2oz) potato flour or cornflour

for serving:
300ml (10fl oz) whipping cream

Tip the chestnut puree into a large mixing bowl. Scoop two rounded tablespoons of the puree onto a saucer and set aside. Stir the vanilla essence and the egg yolks into the puree.

In a separate bowl, whisk the egg whites until stiff. Gradually fold the meringue into the chestnut mixture alternately with the sieved flour. When well combined pour the mixture into the prepared cake tin.

Bake in a preheated oven until the cake is just starting to shrink from the tin. Cool in the tin for 10 minutes then unclip and remove the side of the tin.

Transfer the warm cake to a flat serving plate. Whisk the cream until thick, fold in the reserved chestnut puree. Spoon the cream over the cake or serve separately.

Brandy Snap Baskets with Cornish Tea Ice Cream

A recent and unexpected find in Cornwall is home-produced tea from the Tregothnan estate, near Truro. Their Earl Grey Tea makes a beautiful ice cream which goes so well in a fragile brandy snap basket. Alternatively fill the baskets with a scoop or two of local, clotted cream ice cream and serve straight away before the brandy snap softens.

Oven: 160°C/Fan 140°C/Gas 3 **Baking time:** 8 minutes **Makes:** 8-10 baskets
Equipment: 2 baking sheets, lined or buttered; wide palette knife; 2 rice bowls or small dishes for shaping the brandy snaps

120g (4oz) butter
120g (4oz) demerara sugar
120g (4oz) golden syrup
120g (4oz) plain flour
1 teaspoon ground ginger
1 teaspoon lemon juice
1 teaspoon brandy

In a medium-sized saucepan, gently heat the butter, sugar and syrup until the butter has melted and the sugar has completely dissolved. Remove from the heat and cool slightly. Mix the sieved flour and ginger into the pan, add the lemon juice and brandy and stir until smooth. Allowing plenty of space for the mixture to spread in the oven, place 2 separate tablespoons on each of the prepared baking sheets.

Bake in the preheated oven until the brandy snaps are a deep amber colour - take care not to overcook or the flavour may be bitter. Cool on the baking sheet for 30 seconds then use a palette knife to carefully lift a brandy snap and line a bowl so that the centre is flat but the sides of the biscuit are fluted in 3-4 loose folds. Shape the other biscuit in the same way while it is still hot. Leave for a few minutes until set into the shape then carefully remove the basket. Repeat with the rest of the mixture. Store the brandy snap baskets in an air-tight container in a fridge or freezer until required.

Cornish Tea Ice Cream

The recipe for this delectable Tregothnan Earl Grey tea ice cream is adapted from a green tea version in 'Ice Creams, Sorbets & Gellati', Caroline and Robin Weir's superlative guide to frozen delights. Serve scoops of the ice cream in Brandy Snap Baskets or in small wine glasses with crisp Almond Tuiles (p141).

4 Tregothnan Earl Grey teabags
300ml (10fl oz) whole milk
4 egg yolks
100g (3½oz) caster sugar
300ml (10fl oz) double cream

Snip off and discard the labels and strings of the tea bags. Measure the milk into a jug and add the teabags, making sure they are immersed - if need be, put a cup or plate on top to keep them below the surface. Cover the jug with a plastic bag and refrigerate overnight, stirring now and again, if possible.

Next day, squeeze all the liquid from the teabags into the milk and discard the bags. In a double boiler or a bowl set over simmering water, heat the milk until almost boiling. Beat the egg yolks with the sugar and stir in the milk. Return the mixture to the double boiler and cook, stirring all the time, until it has thickened to a thin custard that coats the back of spoon. Take care not to overcook which might scramble the yolks and spoil the custard.

Cool the custard by standing the bowl, or the upper part of the double boiler, in shallow cold water. Stir now and again until cool. Whisk the cream until thick but still glossy. Gently stir the cream with a balloon whisk while slowly adding the custard. When well combined, pour the ice cream into a lidded plastic box and freeze until firm.

Allow the frozen ice cream to soften slightly in a refrigerator for 30 minutes before serving spoonfuls in the Brandy Snap Baskets.

Rose Geranium Leaf Cake

Visitors to Cornwall sometimes remark on how the geraniums on cottage windowsills often bloom all winter, as they benefit from the warmth of the sun while protected from chill winds by the glass panes. Even small-flowered, scented-leaf geraniums such as the delightful, rose-scented variety provide plenty of young leaves all year round for perfuming a cake. This single-layer Victoria sponge cake is at its buttery best when served warm not long after baking.

Oven: 180°C/Fan 160°C/Gas 4 **Baking time:** 30 minutes **Makes:** 8-10 portion cake
Equipment: 20cm (8in.) spring-clip tin, buttered and base-lined

175g (6oz) butter, at room temperature
175g (6oz) caster sugar
3 eggs
175g (6oz) self-raising flour
5-6 fresh rose-geranium leaves
1 teaspoon rose water

Cream the butter with the sugar until the mixture is pale and fluffy. Add the eggs one at a time, beating them in well. Gradually fold in the sifted flour. Arrange the geranium leaves in the base of the prepared tin with the base of each leaf towards the side of the tin. Spoon the mixture on top of the leaves taking care not to dislodge them and smooth it level.

Bake in the preheated oven until the cake is golden brown and just starting to shrink from the tin. Cool in the tin for 2 minutes then unclip the side of the tin, place a cooling rack over the cake and turn it upside down on to the rack. Remove the base of the tin and carefully peel off the paper to reveal the geranium leaves. Sprinkle the rose water over the cake and serve, cut into portions each with some part of a leaf, while still warm. The geranium leaves are edible though it is perfectly acceptable to remove each piece before eating the cake.

Autumn Harvest Crumble Cake

As summer fades, a late harvest of ripe fruit can often be found in hedgerows and gardens - dark red plums, blueberries, raspberries, early apples, and juicy blackberries. This crumble-topped cake makes a virtue of such autumn bounty though larger fruit should be sliced or cut into small pieces to shorten their cooking times. Crushed amaretti biscuits and flaked almonds form the crumble - a satisfyingly crisp foil to the baked fruit. The cake is nicest served warm with crème fraîche or vanilla ice cream.

Oven: 180°C/Fan 160°C/Gas 4 **Baking time:** 45-50 minutes **Makes:** 8-10 portion cake
Equipment: 23cm (9in.) spring-clip tin, buttered and base-lined

175g (6oz) butter
175g (6oz) golden caster sugar
3 eggs
2 teaspoons orange flower water
200g (7oz) self-raising flour
500g (1lb 2oz) fresh ripe fruit
almond crumble:
100g (3½oz) amaretti biscuits
30g (1oz) flaked almonds
30g (1oz) demerara sugar
60 g (2oz) butter, melted

Blend the butter with the sugar and beat together until pale and fluffy. Mix in the eggs one at a time, beating them in well with the orange flower water. Fold in the sifted flour. Spoon mixture into the prepared cake tin and smooth level. Arrange the fruit on top in a single layer.

Crumble the amaretti biscuits into a bowl and mix in the almonds and sugar. Pour on the melted butter and stir until combined. Sprinkle the crumble mixture over the fruit.

Bake in the preheated oven until a slim bamboo skewer comes out clean from the centre of the cake. Cool in the tin for 5 minutes then unclip and remove the side of the cake tin. Slide the cake onto a flat plate or board and serve straight away.

Figgy Hobbin

Recipes for this Cornish pastry - also known as Figgy 'Obbin - vary widely. Though none include figs since figgy or figgie is an old word for raisins. Victorian recipes specify muscatel raisins that required deseeding before use in cooking. Caramel-flavoured muscatel raisins are hard to find these days so I use seedless raisins and add a little soft brown sugar to compensate. In the past, a suet crust, sometimes with added lard, featured but butter now often replaces both these fats. The recipe below is slightly adapted from a 1960s version from the Cornwall Women's Institute and has an excellent flavour. The pastry is rolled around the raisin filling which gives each slice an attractive spiral of sweet raisins.

Oven: 200°C/Fan 180°C/Gas 6 **Baking time:** 30-40 minutes **Makes:** 12-16 slices
Equipment: baking sheet, greased

230g (8oz) flour
1 teaspoon baking powder
30g (1oz) caster sugar
120g (4oz) butter
5-6 tablespoons milk
grated zest of ½ lemon
175g (6oz) seedless raisins
1 tablespoon light soft brown sugar

Sift the flour and baking powder into a bowl and stir in the sugar. Rub in the butter until the mixture resembles breadcrumbs and mix to a dough with almost all the milk. On a floured board roll out the pastry to a rectangle about 30 x 20cm (12 x 8in.) Sprinkle the lemon zest, raisins, and brown sugar over the pastry leaving a margin each side. Press the filling lightly into the pastry with a rolling pin. Brush the margin with milk and roll up the pastry from the short side.

Transfer the pastry roll, with the end underneath, to the baking sheet. Brush the top with a little milk and lightly mark criss-cross lines with a blunt knife. Bake in the preheated oven until golden brown. Cool the Figgy 'Obbin on a wire rack and then transfer to a bread board or flat plate to cut into slices.

Honey and Walnut Cakes

Individual cakes in paper cases and rich with honey, vanilla, and chopped walnuts. Home-made vanilla essence is simple to make and tastes superb: slice a vanilla pod in half lengthways, then snip into short pieces to feed into a small screw-top jar. Pour in sherry or brandy to cover and seal tightly. Shake vigorously to extract the full flavour and seeds from the pod then store in a dark cupboard and use as required.

Oven: 180°C/Fan 160°C/Gas 4 **Baking time:** 20-25 minutes **Makes:** 18 cakes
Equipment: patty tins, lined with paper cases

120g (4oz) butter
120g (4oz) light muscovado sugar
2 tablespoons clear honey
2 eggs
2 teaspoons home-made vanilla essence or 1 teaspoon vanilla bean paste
150g (5oz) self-raising flour
90g (3oz) broken walnuts, coarsely chopped
18 walnut halves
1 teaspoon icing sugar

Cream the butter with the sugar and honey until light. Beat in the eggs separately with the vanilla essence. Mix in the sifted flour and chopped walnuts. Place a well-rounded dessertspoon of mixture in each paper case and place a walnut half on top of each.

Bake in the preheated oven until golden-brown. Cool slightly then transfer to a wire rack and dust very lightly with sieved icing sugar.

Congress Tarts

In her fine book, Gourmet Cornwall, Carol Trewin writes that Congress Tarts - small pastries with an almond filling and covered with glace icing - are particularly popular in the county.

Oven: 190°C/Fan 170°C/Gas 5 **Baking time:** 20 minutes **Makes:** 12 tarts
Equipment: 7.5cm (3in.) fluted pastry cutter; patty tins, buttered

Pastry:
175g (6oz) plain flour
90g (3oz) butter
2-3 tablespoons milk or water

Filling:
30g (1oz) butter
90g (3oz) caster sugar
1 egg
drop of almond essence
45g (1½oz) ground rice
45g (1½oz) ground almonds
1-2 tablespoons raspberry or strawberry jam

Glace Icing:
60g (2oz) icing sugar
1 tablespoon hot water
few strips of angelica for decoration

Sieve the flour into a bowl and rub in the butter until the mixture resembles breadcrumbs. Mix to a dough with the milk or water. Form the dough into a ball and rest it under the upturned bowl while you prepare the filling for the tarts.

Cream the butter with the sugar and beat in the egg and almond essence until smooth. Fold in the ground rice and ground almonds.

On a floured board, roll out the pastry until 3mm (⅛in.) thick, and cut out 12 rounds to line the prepared patty tins. Place a coffee-spoon of jam in the base of each and cover with a heaped teaspoonful of the almond mixture.

Bake in the preheated oven until the filling is risen and golden brown. Cool in the tin for 3 minutes then transfer to a wire rack. To ice the tarts, blend the sieved icing sugar with just enough hot water to make a pouring consistency, and spoon over the top of each tart. Decorate with a sliver of angelica and leave in a warm kitchen until set.

Triple Ice Cream Marble Cake

An easy and excellent celebration ice cream cake assembled with three different ice creams - home-made or bought - and encased in sponge fingers (also known as boudoir biscuits) flavoured with liqueur or fruit juice. In the summer, I prefer fruit-based ice creams such as cherry, apricot with toasted almond, and passion fruit. For a winter party, chocolate, coffee, and vanilla clotted cream ice creams go well together. Another virtue of this unusual cake is that it can be served outside, even on a hot day, since the sponge fingers help to slow the ice cream from melting.

Makes: 15-20 portion cake
Equipment: 18cm (7in.) square x 7.5cm (3in.) deep cake tin, brushed with sunflower oil and lined with cling film; 20cm (8in.) square baking paper

1.75l (3pts.) ice cream, in 3 different flavours
3 tablespoons Cointreau or other fruit flavoured liqueur
6 tablespoons pear, peach or orange juice
1 tablespoon caster sugar
30-35 sponge fingers
300ml (10fl oz) whipping cream
for decoration (optional):
toasted flaked almonds or grated chocolate

Place the 3 ice creams in a fridge to soften slightly while you prepare the biscuit layer.

In a shallow dish stir together the liqueur with the fruit juice and sugar. Cut a short piece from the ends of 2 sponge fingers so that, cut ends together, they fit into the base of the tin. Dip the non-sugar side of each biscuit in the fruit liquid and place sugar-side down in the base of the tin. Repeat until the base is lined with the biscuits. Now line the sides of the tin by cutting the rest of the biscuits in half. One at a time, dip each half biscuit in the liquid and place sugar-side to the tin with the cut end almost level with its rim. Repeat until the cake tin is lined with the biscuits.

Remove the ice creams from the fridge and use a dessertspoon to place heaps across the base of the tin, varying the colours as in a conventional marble cake. Repeat with more layers until the cake tin is a little more than full. Place the baking paper and a wooden board on top of the cake tin and press down gently to remove air pockets between the spoonfuls of ice cream. Remove the board and freeze the cake until firm.

To remove the cake from the tin, discard the paper and place the tin upside down on a flat serving dish. Wrap a hot damp cloth over the base and sides of the tin and after 2-3 minutes the tin should lift off the cake quite easily. Carefully peel off the food film and discard.

Whisk the cream until thick and place (or pipe if you prefer) spoonfuls along the join in the biscuits on top of the cake and around the base to cover the cut ends. Sprinkle toasted almonds or grated chocolate over the cream and replace in the freezer - unwrapped if serving a few hours later - until needed. Cut the cake into long slices and divide into smaller portions for serving.

Hot Blackberry Cake

Simple to make and ideal for baking at the weekend or on holiday; freshly-gathered blackberries are mixed into a cinnamon-speckled cake which is served straight from the oven with local ice cream. If short of blackberries make up the weight with diced, ripe pear.

Oven: 180°C/Fan 160°C/Gas 4 **Baking time:** 35-40 minutes **Makes:** 12-16 portion cake
Equipment: 20cm (8in.) square tin, buttered

230g (8oz) ripe, juicy blackberries
2 tablespoon clear honey
230g (8oz) self-raising flour
120g (4oz) caster sugar
¼ teaspoon ground cinnamon
120g (4 oz) butter, frozen or chilled
1 egg, beaten
6-8 tablespoons milk

Rinse the blackberries in cold water then drain them well on kitchen paper. Tip the fruit into a bowl and stir in the honey until the blackberries are evenly coated.

In a mixing bowl, measure in the flour, sugar and cinnamon. Stir together then grate in the butter. Mix in the beaten egg and half the milk with the blackberries. Add more milk, if necessary, to make a soft mixture. Spoon the mixture into the prepared tin and smooth more or less level.

Bake the cake in the preheated oven until a bamboo skewer comes out clean from the centre. Cool the cake in the tin for a few minutes then cut into portions and serve with cream or ice cream.

Easter Biscuits

Traditionally baked for Easter Sunday tea-time, these spiced biscuits are, however, enjoyable all year round.

Oven: 180°C/Fan 160°C/Gas 4 **Baking time:** 15 minutes **Makes:** about 20 biscuits
Equipment: 7.5cm (3in.) fluted pastry cutter; baking sheet, lined or buttered

120g (4oz) butter
120g (4oz) caster sugar
1 small egg
230g (8oz) plain flour
1 teaspoon ground mixed spice
60g (2oz) currants
a little beaten egg white for glazing biscuits
for decoration:
1 tablespoon golden or white granulated sugar

Cream the butter with the sugar then beat in the egg. Gradually work in the flour sieved with the spice, and then the currants. Knead lightly with the fingertips to make a soft dough and shape into a ball.

On a lightly-floured board roll out the dough until 0.5cm (¼ in.) thick. Cut out the biscuits with the cutter. Transfer the biscuits to the prepared baking sheet, brush lightly with beaten egg white and sprinkle with a little granulated sugar.

Bake in the preheated oven until the biscuits are pale gold but take care not to overcook. Cool on the baking sheet for a few minutes then transfer to a wire rack.

West Country Cream Tea

A freshly-brewed pot of tea with milk, sugar, and pretty teacups, a plate of warm scones or Cornish splits and a gleaming jar of strawberry jam with a generous dish of thick golden-yellow clotted cream; these are the ingredients of a genuine cream tea. There may also be a home-made cake and tempting sandwiches - paper-thin cucumber with a smidgeon of Gentlemen's Relish, smoked salmon triangles, and local asparagus rolled in brown bread and butter. What pleasure to share such modest luxury for an hour or two with friends or family, a blissful respite from a hurried world.

This simple yet delightful afternoon event is served throughout the West Country. But it is the counties of Devon and Cornwall that lay claim to the the origin of the fabled cream tea. In 1775 the Reverend William Gilpin, visiting Cotehele, near Saltash in Cornwall, wrote that he was served a local cream tea: 'Here we refreshed ourselves with tea, and larded our bread, after the fashion of the county, with clouted cream.' Nowadays this light meal is widely available - in teashops, in National Trust gardens, in pubs, and hotels - ideally with a terrace overlooking the sea. And some of us also serve cream teas in the comfort of our own homes.

The English fashion for afternoon tea probably began in 1840 when the Duchess of Bedford declared that drinking tea with a little refreshment saved her from 'that sinking feeling' in the long interval between luncheon and dinner. Yet, in France more than a century earlier, Madame de Sévigné had referred to the custom in a letter to a friend as 'le thé de cinq heures'.

Cornish devotees of the cream tea are keen to point out their preference for yeast-leavened splits as the basis for strawberry jam with clotted cream and, they emphasise, spooned on in that order. Devon can parry with their own 'chudleigh' - also yeast-leavened and cut across - but with the clotted cream layer first then topped with jam. Cornwall also boasts an unusual and fine-tasting variation known as 'Thunder and Lightning' when black treacle takes the place of jam - though clotted cream is, of course, still essential. In Somerset and Dorset, however, the freshly-baked scone holds sway, and it appears that the order in which you ladle on the jam and cream is simply a matter of personal preference.

The rapid growth of tourism in the West Country that followed the arrival of the railway in the nineteenth century has boosted the popularity of cream teas not just throughout the United Kingdom but further afield too. I've been offered a mile-high version - complete with Cornish clotted cream - halfway across the Atlantic, and in a hotel on Victoria Island off Vancouver, afternoon tea is served all day long. But as far as I know, in the beautiful counties where the custom arose, a cream tea is only really acceptable at its traditional time, as the sun begins to dip slowly in the western sky.

Whoever invented clotted cream deserves a medal, or several. What began as a clever way to prevent the deterioration of dairy cream before the days of refrigeration gave rise to a superb and unique product - thick, butter-yellow clotted cream with its characteristic puckered crust and delicately caramelised flavour. Though clotted cream is produced in the West Country, it is now appreciated all over the British Isles and in many countries abroad.

Some historians have suggested that this method of preservation has been practised for at least 2000 years in the Middle East, Iran and India, using buffalo milk, and was introduced into Cornwall by Phoenician merchants trading for the county's valuable tin ore. By gently heating the cream skimmed from fresh non-homogenised cow's milk, usually from Channel Island breeds, the butterfat is concentrated to a minimum of 55% which extends the life of fresh cream and increases its value. There might be no medal for the person who discovered the method but recognition for Cornish clotted cream arrived in 1998 when it was awarded the Protected Designation of Origin status by the European Union.

Clotted cream has been produced in Cornwall and Devon for centuries and along with eggs, butter and milk, was taken each week by horse-drawn cart to be sold at local markets and in dairy shops. On the side of a building in Bath there is still an old advertisement for high-quality dairy produce supplied by Devon farmers.

But it was the arrival of the railway during the reign of Queen Victoria that boosted the sale and renown of clotted cream. Butter and cream taken by an evening train to London could be on the capital's breakfast tables soon after dawn. During the summer months, the trains returned with thousands of holiday makers from all over Britain, keen to discover the beauty of the West Country. Naturally, they were eager to consume the local specialities and the sale of clotted cream shot up. And its remarkable keeping quality enabled holidaymakers to send by post presents of small tins of fresh clotted cream to friends and family at home.

Some years ago, at a time of agricultural milk quotas in Devon, I made clotted cream at home following a recipe from the Cornwall Women's Institute. It's not a difficult process but benefits from a sharp eye, a steady hand and a patient nature.

Clotted Cream

Pour 2 litres (3-4 pints) of fresh, whole milk - pasteurised but not homogenised - into a glass jug or bowl and leave in a cold place overnight.

Next day use a ladle to remove the yellow cream on top of the milk to a china basin with sloping sides. Place the basin in a saucepan half-filled with warm water and heat very gently until it reaches 82°C (180°F.) Keep the water at this temperature for 1-2 hours or until the surface of the cream is uneven with a deeper yellow crust. Very gently, lift the bowl from the saucepan and leave it in a cold place until morning.

Then use a flat slotted spoon, known as a creamer or skimmer, to carefully lift off the more solid cream and slide it into a serving dish. The milk beneath the cream is highly recommended for making cakes and scones.

Fresh Strawberry Jam

An uncooked and 'instant' jam which is delicious served with freshly-baked scones and clotted cream. The raspberry version is equally good.

230g (8oz) ripe strawberries or raspberries
2-4 tablespoons caster sugar
½ orange, finely grated zest and juice

Mash the fruit with a fork and work in the sugar and the zest and strained juice of the orange. Alternatively, crush the ingredients together in a blender or processor but for only a brief time, and well before the mixture becomes too runny. Spoon the jam into a small dish and serve.

Cake Stall Plain Scones

Every week, I baked scores of these scones - an essential component of a Devon cream tea - for my Tiverton cake stall. By some people's reckoning they are not totally plain scones since I include butter, sugar and eggs in my recipe. The result, however, is so much more delicious than the all-too-solid, floury versions often encountered. The dried fruit version is also given below.

Oven: 220°C/Fan 200°F/Gas 7 **Baking time:** 12-15 minutes **Makes:** about 12 scones
Equipment: 5cm (2 in.) fluted pastry cutter, baking sheet lightly floured

230g (8oz) self-raising flour
1 teaspoon baking powder
good pinch salt
45g (1½oz) caster sugar
60g (2oz) butter
1 egg lightly whisked with milk to make 150ml (5fl oz)
glaze: egg yolk blended with a little cream or milk

Sift the flour, baking powder, salt and sugar into a mixing bowl. Add the butter in pieces and rub in with the fingertips until the mixture resembles breadcrumbs. Add the egg and milk while mixing with a knife to form a soft dough.

Turn the dough onto a well-floured board and press lightly into a flat, round shape. Dust a little flour over the dough and pat or gently roll out until 1 cm (½ in.) thick. Dip the pastry cutter into some flour and using a firm downward movement, cut out as many scones from the dough as you can. Knead together the trimmings and cut out more circles. Place the scones on the prepared baking sheet and brush the tops with the egg yolk glaze.

Bake in the preheated oven until well-risen with a golden-brown crust. Cool on the baking sheet for 2 minutes then transfer to a cloth-lined plate or basket and serve while still hot.

Fruit Scones
Add 60g (2oz) seedless raisins or sultanas to the dry ingredients in the recipe for *Plain Scones*, then follow the same method, allowing an extra 1-2 minutes baking time.

Cornish Splits & Devonshire Chudleighs

Cornwall is renowned for these yeast-risen, flat baps, sometimes known as tuffs, which are indeed split open and served with plenty of strawberry jam and clotted cream as the essential element in a traditional cream tea. A similar but smaller version of Cornish splits is made across the Tamar where Devonshire splits are also known as Chudleighs.

Oven: 200°C/Fan 180°C/Gas 6 **Baking time:** 15-20 minutes **Makes:** 12 splits
Equipment: 2 baking sheets, floured

450g (1lb) flour
1½ teaspoons dried yeast
300ml (10fl oz) milk
60g (2oz) butter
1 teaspoon sugar
½ teaspoon salt
a little extra milk

Measure the flour and dried yeast into a bowl. Carefully warm the milk with the butter, sugar and salt until melted and dissolved. Check that the temperature is warm not hot then pour the liquid into the flour and stir until well mixed.

Turn the dough out onto a floured surface and knead lightly for 3-5 minutes until the dough begins to feel elastic. Replace the dough in the bowl, cover with a cloth and leave in a warm place until the dough has doubled in size. Transfer the dough to a floured surface and knead lightly for 2-3 minutes. Cut into 12 pieces and shape each one into a ball. Slightly flatten the splits onto the prepared baking sheet placing them about 2cm (1in.) apart. Leave the baking sheet in a warm draught-proof place for the dough to rise and the splits are touching.

Lightly brush the tops of the splits with the extra milk and bake in the preheated oven until the tops are golden brown. Cool the splits on the baking sheet for a few minutes then gently tear the splits apart and serve.

Devonshire

From the top of Dippy Orchard you could look across the cider apple trees and down the grassy slope, to where the sheep and geese grazed, to the long thatched roof and curved cobb walls of what was our family home for more than twenty years. It was here, in the large, warm kitchen overlooking the garden that I began to bake in earnest; all day and every day, producing hundreds of cakes, large and small. There were scones and tarts, meringues and macaroons, cookies and biscuits, all carefully placed into my little yellow car. Then, in time-honoured custom, I transported them twelve miles through the narrow lanes to Tiverton Pannier Market where I launched my own independent cake stall, which ran for twelve months, allowing me time to embrace all the seasons, feasts and festivals of the area.

The kitchen had a flagstone floor, with a deep well in the corner where you could see the fresh spring water running fifty feet below. Opposite was an inglenook fireplace and to one side there was a brick bread oven with a metal door to contain the heat. In the next room was another inglenook fireplace with a curved brick alcove where a cloam oven once rested, heated by a flue from the back of the open fire. As I mixed the cakes and baked them in my modern electric oven, I pondered on the skill and patience of Devonshire home bakers who had lived there before me. How had they baked Braunton Revel Buns, Devonshire Fruit Loaf, and other bygone recipes in this book, before the arrival of gas and electricity?

Historically farmhouse baking in a brick or stone bread-oven was usually a weekly task, beginning early in the morning when bundles of brushwood or furze would be lit; the fire would burn brightly, smoke billowing up the chimney and through the wide doorway to the yard. Only when the little pebble, embedded in the floor at the front of the oven, had changed colour was the temperature high enough to bake your bread, which would be waiting, kneaded and ready after proving overnight. As soon as the crusty loaves were withdrawn from the oven, a batch of yeast-risen cakes and buns went in and the heavy metal door would be closed once more. In times of plenty, a fruit cake or a cider cake would also be prepared, ready to slide into the oven when the temperature had dropped low enough. Following that, there would be some Cattern cakes or gingerbread, or a delicate egg and cream custard, all slowly baked in the dying heat of the bread oven. Finally, while the results of the day's work were cooling on the kitchen table, the tired cook could rest for a while, satisfied that there was enough splendid baking for the week ahead.

Compared with the rigours of the past, and using our labour-saving equipment to mix and bake, it is easy for us to make a cake or scones or biscuits. Yet we are still able to share in the experience of earlier generations; what for them was a necessity, is now an enjoyable choice - the pleasure of using local ingredients: eggs and honey, butter and flour, cream and soft fruit. And so our home baking, like theirs, truly reflects where we live.

Recipes for Devonshire

52 Devonshire Fruit Loaf
53 Sidmouth Wholemeal Scones
54 Braunton Revel Buns
56 Beekeeper's Honey Cake
57 Cider Cake
58 Chocolate Cake filled with Devon cream
60 Wholewheat Sponge Cake with Fudge Filling
62 Orange Sponge Cake with Citrus Curd
64 Chocolate Cranberry Cake with Yoghurt Frosting
66 Clyst William Barton Cake
67 Otterton Mill Gingerbread
68 Rose Petal Sponge Cake with Rose Petal Cream
70 Honiton Cattern Cakes
72 Lime Curd Tarts
73 Chocolate Coconut Squares
74 Hot Strawberry Tarts
76 Devon Blizzard Cake
78 Apple Sauce Cake
80 Plymtree Harvest Cake
81 Devon Apple Butter

Devonshire Fruit Loaf

Home-made, yeast-risen, fruit loaves are particularly delicious. The advantage of making two smaller loaves, rather than a large one, is that the second can be saved for a few days later, or it can be wrapped and stored in the freezer for longer.

Oven: 200°C/Fan 180°C/Gas 6 **Baking time:** 45-50 minutes **Makes:** two 500g (1lb) loaves
Equipment: two 500g (1lb) loaf tins, buttered and base-lined

¼ teaspoon dried saffron threads
60ml (2fl oz) warm water
500g (1lb 2oz) flour
7g (¼oz) fast-action dried yeast
½ teaspoon ground nutmeg
60g (2oz) caster sugar
300g (10oz) dried mixed fruit and candied peel
60g (2oz) butter
300ml (10fl oz) warm milk
extra warm water for mixing
½ teaspoon clear honey

Use scissors to chop the saffron threads into small pieces then soak the spice in a cup with the warm water and leave overnight or place briefly in a microwave oven on low to release the colour and flavour into the water.

In a large bowl, mix together the flour, yeast, nutmeg, sugar and dried fruit. Melt the butter in the milk and add the saffron liquid with the threads. Pour onto the flour mixture and add enough warm water to mix to a sticky dough. Mix well for 3-4 minutes. Cover the bowl with a clean cloth and leave in a warm place for 1-2 hours or until the mixture has doubled in size.

Transfer the dough to a lightly floured board and knead lightly for 1-2 minutes. Divide in half, knead each piece into an oval shape and place in the prepared loaf tins. Leave to prove in a warm place for 1 hour or until the tops of the loaves are above the edge of the tins.

Bake in the preheated oven until golden brown and the bottom of each loaf gives a hollow sound when tapped. Cool the loaves on a wire rack and brush the honey over the top crust.

Sidmouth Wholemeal Scones

Triangular wholemeal scones, studded with pecan nuts, which go well with soup or salad as an alternative to a loaf of bread.

Oven: 220°C/Fan 200°C/Gas 7 **Baking time:** 10-15 minutes **Makes:** 12 scones
Equipment: large baking sheet, buttered and lightly floured

230g (8oz) self-raising wholemeal flour
pinch of salt
90g (3oz) butter
30g (1oz) pecan nuts, chopped
1 egg
100ml (3½fl oz) milk, buttermilk or yoghurt
12 pecan nut halves

Sift the flour and salt into a bowl then tip in the bran left in the sieve. Add the butter in pieces and rub in until the mixture resembles breadcrumbs then stir in the chopped nuts. Beat the egg with the milk, reserve a little for brushing the tops of the scones and stir the rest into the mixture to make a soft dough.

Turn out onto a floured board and pat or gently roll into an oblong shape about 2cm (¾ in.) thick. Use a palette knife to cut into 12 triangle-shape scones. Brush the tops with the reserved egg mixture and press a pecan nut on to each one.

Bake in the preheated oven until golden-brown and serve while still warm.

Braunton Revel Buns

Revelry we know. But 'A Revel', according to Florence White, was an anniversary feast to celebrate the dedication of a church or chapel. Given the number of nineteenth century chapels in north Devon, home-bakers must have been pretty busy producing buns for all those chapel teas. These rich, yeast-leavened buns have a cake-like texture and they are not only delicious to eat but also fun to make; collecting fresh sycamore leaves for placing under each bun and watching how saffron yields its unique flavour and colour in warm milk. For the best results leave the dough to prove overnight in a warm place.

Oven: 200°C/Fan 180°C/Gas 6 **Baking time:** 20-25 minutes **Makes:** 24 large or 48 small buns
Equipment: 2-3 baking sheets, floured; 24 fresh sycamore leaves - optional

½ teaspoon or generous pinch of saffron
150ml (5fl oz) milk
425ml (15fl oz) single cream
700g (1lb 8oz) white bread flour
230g (8oz) butter
230g (8oz) caster sugar
1 teaspoon ground cinnamon
15g (½oz) rapid-rise dried yeast
230g (8oz) currants
1 egg, beaten
1 tablespoon icing or caster sugar

Use scissors to snip the strands of saffron into small pieces and add to the milk in a pan. Leave over very low heat, stirring now and again for 30 minutes or longer, until the saffron has coloured the milk a beautiful yellow. Add the cream to the milk and stir until warm then remove from the heat.

Measure the flour into a large mixing bowl and rub in the butter. Stir in the sugar, cinnamon, dried yeast and currants. Use a large wooden spoon to stir in the beaten egg and saffron-rich milk and cream. Mix until well combined and the dough is sticky and starting to become elastic.

Scrape all the dough into the base of the bowl, cover the bowl with a clean tea-cloth and leave in a warm place until doubled in size, ideally overnight.

Remove the stalks and arrange the sycamore leaves, underside-up, on the baking sheets. Scoop a heaped tablespoon of the dough, weighing about 60g (2oz), on to a lightly floured board and shape into a ball. Place each ball of dough on a sycamore leaf pressing down lightly so that the ribbed pattern of the leaf is impressed on the underside of the bun. If making smaller buns, shape rounded dessertspoons, weighing about 30g (1oz), of the mixture into balls and place on the prepared baking sheets. Leave the buns in a warm place for about 45 minutes or until puffy.

Bake the buns in the preheated oven until risen and golden brown. Cool on a wire rack then carefully remove the sycamore leaves and dust the buns with sieved icing or caster sugar.

Beekeeper's Honey Cake

When I kept bees, the enjoyable monthly meetings of the Devon Beekeepers' Association were held in Broadclyst. Knowing my interest in baking, one of the members gave me the recipe for this easy-to-make and excellent cake and since its appearance in BBC Good Food the cake has become popular way beyond the West Country.

Oven: 180°C/Fan 160°C/Gas 4 **Baking time:** 45 minutes **Makes:** 8 portion cake
Equipment: 18-20cm (7-8 in.) tin, buttered and base-lined

150g (5oz) butter
100g (3½oz) light muscovado sugar
175g (6oz) honey
1 tablespoon water
2 eggs
200g (7oz) self-raising flour

Icing:
120g (4oz) icing sugar
1 tablespoon clear honey
1 tablespoon water

In a medium-size saucepan, gently heat the butter, sugar and honey with the water until the butter has melted. Immediately remove from the heat and beat in the eggs and the sifted flour. Pour the mixture into the prepared cake tin.

Bake in the preheated oven until the cake is just starting to shrink from the tin. Cool the cake in the tin and ice while still warm. Or turn the cake onto a wire rack and leave until cold.

For the icing, sift the icing sugar into a bowl. Stir in the honey and water and mix until smooth. Trickle the icing over the cake in a trellis pattern.

Cider Cake

Local cider contributes a pleasing, subtle flavour to this cake. The original recipe, entitled Old English Cider Cake was published fifty years ago by the Devon Women's Institute with the advice to leave the cake until the following day before cutting. I have added chopped candied peel - ideally home-made - to the mixture which contributes a complementary flavour and contrasting texture to the cake.

Oven: 180°C/Fan 160°C/Gas 4 **Baking time:** 40-45 minutes **Makes:** 16 portion cake
Equipment: 20cm (8in.) square shallow cake tin, base-lined

230g (8oz) flour
½ teaspoon bicarbonate of soda
½ teaspoon ground ginger
½ teaspoon grated nutmeg
120g (4oz) butter
120g (4oz) caster
2 eggs
120g (4oz) candied peel, chopped
150ml (5fl oz) cider
1 tablespoon clear honey

Sift together the flour with bicarbonate of soda and the spices onto a plate. Cream the butter with the sugar until light and fluffy. Beat in the eggs, one at a time. Add the candied peel and mix in the flour mixture with the cider until well combined. Spoon the mixture into the prepared tin and spread level.

Bake the cake in the preheated oven until the cake is starting to shrink from the tin and a slim bamboo skewer comes out clean from the centre. Remove from the oven and brush honey over the top of the cake. Leave the cake to cool in the tin and cut into portions on the following day. I prefer to serve the cake warm, just heat in a microwave oven for a minute or so.

Chocolate Cake Filled With Devon Cream

One of the most popular cakes on my cake stall and still a family favourite. The sponge cake is sandwiched with whipped cream and topped with smooth chocolate frosting.

Oven: 180°C/Fan 160°C/Gas 4 **Baking time:** 30-35 minutes **Makes:** 8 portion cake
Equipment: two 20cm (8in.) sponge sandwich tins, buttered and base-lined

60g (2oz) cocoa
6 tablespoon hot water
175g (6oz) butter
175g (6oz) light muscovado sugar, sieved
175g (6oz) self-raising flour
1 teaspoon baking powder
pinch ground cinnamon
3 eggs

Filling:
150ml (5fl oz) double cream

Frosting:
90g (3oz) icing sugar
30g (1oz) cocoa powder
60g (2oz) light muscovado sugar
60g (2oz) butter
2 tablespoons water

In a mixing bowl, blend the cocoa with the hot water until smooth. Add the butter in pieces and all the remaining ingredients: sugar, flour, baking powder, cinnamon and eggs. Mix together for 2-3 minutes, ideally using a hand-held electric beater, until completely smooth.

Divide the mixture between the prepared cake tins and smooth level. Bake in the preheated oven until the middle of the cake is springy to the touch and it is just starting to shrink from the tin. Cool in the cake tins for 3 minutes then turn the cakes out onto a wire rack to cool.

Whisk the cream until thick but still glossy, if you wish to sweeten the cream stir in a teaspoon of caster sugar. Spoon the cream over one of the cakes and place the other on top.

Make the chocolate frosting by sieving the icing sugar and cocoa into a bowl. Measure the muscovado sugar, butter and water into a small pan and stir over low heat until dissolved, then bring to the boil. Remove from the heat, cool for 1 minute then pour onto the sugar/cocoa mixture and beat until smooth. Pour the frosting over the cake allowing it to trickle down the sides. Leave the cake in a cool place for 2 hours to set.

Variation: melted chocolate is an alternative to the frosting. Break 100g (3½oz) plain dessert chocolate into pieces in a bowl. Add a small knob of butter or 2 tablespoons of cream and melt in a microwave oven or by placing the bowl over simmering water. Gently stir until smooth and spread over the cake then set aside until dry.

Whole-Wheat Sponge Cake With Fudge Filling

When Desna Greenhow restored Otterton Mill, near Budleigh Salterton, in the 1980s, my friend Doreen Chetwood, a life-long champion of baking with wholemeal flour, helped to develop recipes including this most agreeable sponge cake.

Oven: 160°C/Fan 140°C/Gas 3 **Baking time:** 30-35 minutes **Makes:** 8 portion cake
Equipment: two 20cm (8 in.) sponge sandwich tins, buttered and base-lined

90g (3oz) light muscovado sugar
1 tablespoon clear honey
¼ teaspoon vanilla essence
4 eggs, separated
4 tablespoons hot water
120g (4oz) plain whole-wheat flour

Fudge Filling:
60g (2oz) butter
120g (4oz) light muscovado sugar
1 tablespoon single cream
1 teaspoon icing sugar

Measure the sugar, honey, vanilla essence, egg yolks and hot water into a bowl. Whisk until light and foamy with an electric beater or food mixer.

In a separate bowl, whisk the egg whites until stiff, then fold into the yolk mixture. Tip the flour into a sieve and shake a fine layer over the mixture. Fold in gently and repeat until only bran remains in the sieve. Fold in half the bran and return the remainder to the flour bag. Divide the cake mixture between the prepared tins and smooth level.

Bake in the preheated oven until the cakes are well-risen and springy to the touch. Cool in the tins for 2 minutes then turn the cakes onto a wire rack to cool.

Make the filling by melting the butter in a pan over moderate heat then stir in the sugar and cream until dissolved. Bring the mixture to the boil and cook for 2 minutes. Remove from the heat and cool the pan by standing it in cold water for 2-3 minutes. Beat the filling until it is thick but still spreadable. Pour the filling over one cake and place the other on top. Lightly dust the cake with sieved icing sugar and leave until the filling is set.

Orange Sponge Cake Filled With Citrus Curd

The mild climate and long hours of sunshine in the West Country make growing a citrus tree perfectly feasible - though preferably in a pot for overwintering in a glass porch or conservatory. So perhaps it's not too fanciful to imagine a superb regional treat of home-grown oranges, lemons and kumquats.

Oven: 180°C/Fan 160°C/Gas 4 **Baking time:** 40-45 minutes **Makes:** 8 portion cake
Equipment: two 18cm (7in.) sponge sandwich tins, buttered and base-lined

120g (4oz) butter
120g (4oz) caster sugar
1 orange or lemon, or 2 clementines; finely grated zest
2 eggs
120g (4oz) self-raising flour

Fruit Curd Filling:
1 orange, lemon, or 2 clementines, finely grated zest and strained juice
60g (2oz) caster sugar
1 egg
¼ teaspoon cornflour
60g (2oz) butter
1 teaspoon icing or caster sugar

Cream the butter and sugar with the fruit zest in a mixing bowl until light and fluffy. Beat in the eggs separately, then fold in the sieved flour. Spoon the mixture into the prepared cake tins and smooth level.

Bake in the preheated oven until golden brown and the cake is just starting to shrink from the tins. Cool the cakes in the tins for 3 minutes then turn out on to a wire rack.

To make the fruit curd: use a glass or ceramic double boiler or place a non-metal bowl over a pan of simmering water. Use a wooden spoon to mix together the fruit zest and juice with the sugar, egg and cornflour over moderate heat until thickened. Take care not to overcook or the curd may become granular with particles of cooked egg. As soon as the mixture is cooked, remove from the heat and stand the pan or bowl in cold water to cool the mixture. When half-cooled, beat in the butter in small pieces until melted.

Sandwich the cake layers with the curd and sift icing or caster sugar over the top of the cake then set aside in a cold place before serving.

Chocolate and Cranberry Cake with Yoghurt Frosting

Chocolate cakes may include unexpected ingredients these days such as beer, chilli pepper, or even carbonated cola drink. In Totnes, I discovered a chocolate cake that contained cooked beetroot, its taste undetectable yet the vegetable helps to contribute a soft crumb with no hint of dryness to the cake. This is my version of a beetroot-enriched chocolate cake with added cranberries and a white frosting in lovely contrast to the dark cake.

Oven: 180°C/Fan 160°C/Gas 4 **Baking time:** 40-45 minutes **Makes:** 16 square portions
Equipment: 23 cm (9 in.) square cake tin - lined

175g (6oz) dried cranberries
1 orange, juice and finely grated zest
230g (8oz) cooked beetroot, peeled
175g (6oz) butter, softened
60g (2oz) cocoa powder
175g (6oz) dark muscovado sugar
3 eggs
175g (6oz) self-raising flour
1 teaspoon baking powder
good pinch ground cinnamon

Frosting:
175g (6oz) icing sugar
2 tablespoons plain natural yoghurt
few drops of vanilla essence

Reserve 1 tablespoon of cranberries for decoration of the cake. Gently heat the rest of the berries in a small pan with the strained juice and zest of orange, stirring now and again. Remove from the heat and cover the pan with a plate until needed. Cut the beetroot into pieces and chop fairly finely in a processor.

Use an electric beater or mixer to blend the butter with the cocoa powder then beat in the sugar, if it's lumpy sieve it first. Mix in the eggs, one at a time, alternately with the beetroot until well combined. Sieve the flour with the baking powder and cinnamon and stir in until well mixed. Finally mix in the cooled cranberries.

Spoon the mixture into the cake tin and smooth level. Bake in the preheated oven until a slim bamboo skewer comes out clean from the centre. Cool the cake in the tin for 5 minutes then gently remove and leave on a wire rack.

To make the frosting, sieve the icing sugar into a bowl and mix in the yoghurt a little at a time to give a spreadable consistency - take care because it's easy to add too much yoghurt. Spread over the top of the cake in an even layer. Chop the reserved cranberries and scatter over the frosting then leave the cake until the frosting has set. Cut into squares for serving.

Clyst William Barton Cake

A fruit cake that I devised using the old method of rubbing the butter into the mixture. Named after the thatched Devon farmhouse that was our family home for many years and which dates from the Domesday Book. Clyst is old English for spring, which fed the well in one corner of the flag-stoned kitchen.

Oven: 160°C/Fan 140°C/Gas 3 **Baking time:** 1½ hours **Makes:** 12 portion cake
Equipment: 1kg (2 lb) loaf tin - buttered and base-lined

300g (10oz) plain flour
175g (6oz) demerara sugar
175g (6oz) butter
400g (14oz) mixed dried fruit - raisins, sultanas, currants
60g (2oz) glacé cherries, quartered
1 teaspoon mixed spice
1 teaspoon baking powder
3 eggs
1 tablespoon black treacle

Measure the flour into a bowl and mix in the sugar. Add the butter in pieces and rub in with your fingertips until the mixture resembles breadcrumbs. Stir in the dried fruit, cherries, spice and baking powder. Beat the eggs with the treacle and mix in well. Spoon the mixture into the prepared cake tin and smooth level.

Bake in the preheated oven until cooked when a slim bamboo skewer comes out clean from the centre of the cake. Cool in the tin for 15 minutes then transfer to a wire rack.

Otterton Mill Gingerbread

Inspired by a recipe from Otterton Mill, this gingerbread, enriched with sultanas and crystallised ginger, is simple to make and has a particularly pleasing flavour.

Oven: 160°C/Fan 140°C/Gas 3 **Baking time:** 45-50 minutes **Makes:** 20 slices
Equipment: 20cm (8 in.) square tin, buttered and base-lined

75ml (2½ fl oz) milk
120g (4oz) butter
120g (4oz) dark muscovado sugar
120g (4oz) black treacle
120g (4oz) golden syrup
2 eggs, beaten
175g (6oz) self-raising flour
120g (4oz) wholemeal self-raising flour
1½ teaspoons ground ginger
½ teaspoon ground cinnamon
½ teaspoon mixed spice
60g (2oz) sultanas
60g (2oz) crystallised ginger, chopped

Heat the milk with the butter in a large saucepan until the butter has melted. Remove from the heat and cool the pan by standing it in shallow, cold water. Add the sugar, treacle and syrup with the eggs and stir until well combined. Mix in both kinds of flour, the spices, sultanas and crystallised ginger. Pour the mixture into the prepared tin and smooth level.

Bake in the preheated oven until the cake is just starting to shrink from the tin and a slim bamboo skewer comes out clean from the centre. Cool the cake in the tin for 15 minutes then transfer to a wire rack. The flavour of the cake is specially good when served warm, either on its own or accompanied by spoonfuls of soured cream.

Rose Petal Sponge Cake With Rose Petal Cream

Some years ago, on a warm summer morning, I gathered all the fresh rose petals from my Devon garden and took them to the local railway station for rapid transit to London where that evening they starred at a banquet held to honour Princess Diana. Perfumed rose petals are a charming and delicate ingredient in this cake, appearing in the rosewater cream and as decoration. With such fragile ingredients this sponge cake is best served the day it is prepared.

Oven: 180°C/Fan 160°C/Gas 4 **Baking time:** 25 minutes **Makes:** 8 portion cake
Equipment: two 19cm (7½ in.) sponge sandwich tins, buttered and base-lined;
sheet of baking paper for the candied rose petals

Candied Rose Petals:
2-3 handfuls of fresh unsprayed pink and red rose petals
1 egg white
a few drops of rosewater
30g (1oz) caster sugar

Sponge Cake:
4 eggs
120g (4oz) caster sugar
120g (4oz) flour
60g (2oz) butter, melted
1 teaspoon rose water

Rose Water Cream:
150ml (5fl oz) whipping cream
1 tablespoon caster sugar
1-2 teaspoons rose water
1-2 drops pink food colouring

Prepare the candied rose petals first: select about 20 of the firmest pink petals. Lightly whisk the egg white with a few drops of rose water and brush both sides of a petal then dust with the caster sugar and place on the baking paper to dry. Repeat with the rest of the selected petals.

Place the remaining petals and remaining sugar in a food processor and chop briefly until you have a fairly fine rose petal mixture for decorating the cake.

To make the cake, whisk the eggs with the caster sugar until foamy and thick enough for the whisk to leave a trail across the top of the mixture. Do this in an electric mixer or use a hand-held electric whisk and place the mixing bowl over a pan of simmering water to speed up the process. Measure the flour into a sieve and dust the top of the mixture with a thin layer then fold in with a balloon whisk, repeat 2-3 times then add the flour alternately with a trickle of melted butter. Fold in gently to lose as little air as possible from the mixture. When the flour and butter have been incorporated, divide the mixture between the prepared cake tins.

Bake in the preheated oven until the cakes are golden brown and just starting to shrink from the tin. Cool in the tins for 3 minutes then turn out on to a wire rack and peel off the lining paper. Sprinkle the rosewater over the cakes and leave until cool.

For the rose petal cream: whisk the cream with the sugar until thick but still glossy and fold in enough rose water to flavour with just a drop of food colouring to make the cream blush pink. Fold in half the rose petal powder, spread the cream over one cake and place the other on top. Sprinkle the rest of the rose petal sugar over the cake and arrange the candied rose petals on top or around the cake. Chill the cake until ready to serve.

Honiton Cattern Cakes

Near the top end of the high street, the Honiton lace shop displays beautiful examples of the famous lace including a portrait of Queen Victoria in her wedding dress. The name Cattern derives from St Catherine, the patron saint of spinners and lace makers, whose emblem is the wheel. These delicately spiced pastries are either spiral shape or plain circles, large or small, marked with the eight spokes of a wheel.

Oven: 190°C/Fan 170°C/Gas 5 **Baking time:** 15-25 minutes depending on size
Makes: 8 portion cake or 18 small cakes **Equipment:** 20cm (8in.) loose-base sponge cake tin or baking sheet, buttered; 5cm (2 in.) fluted biscuit cutter

120g (4oz) self-raising flour
¼ teaspoon ground cinnamon
75g (2½ oz) caster sugar
30g (1oz ground almonds
30g (1oz) seedless raisins
30g (1oz) currants
90g (3oz) butter
1 egg, beaten

Sift the flour and ground cinnamon into a bowl and stir in the sugar, ground almonds and dried fruit. Melt the butter and add to the bowl with the egg and mix to a stiff dough. Shape the dough into a ball.

For one large Cattern Cake: roll out the pastry to make a 15cm (6in.) circle. Transfer to the prepared cake tin and flatten the pastry with your fingers and the palm of your hand to fit the tin. Mark the edge of the pastry with the handle of a spoon and use a blunt knife to mark 8 spokes of the wheel.

Bake in the preheated oven until golden-brown. Cool in the tin, then cut through into 8 portions and transfer to a serving plate.

For spiral Cattern Cakes: roll out the ball of pastry until 0.5cm (¼ in.) thick and cut the pastry into 0.5cm (¼ in.) wide strips and curl each one into a spiral shape. Use a palette knife to transfer to the prepared baking sheet, allowing room for the pastry to spread.

For small round Cattern Cakes: roll out the pastry until 0.5cm (¼ in.) thick and cut out cakes with the biscuit cutter. Transfer them to the prepared baking sheet, allowing room for the pastry to spread. Mark spokes on each one with a sharp knife.

Bake both spiral and small cakes in the preheated oven until the cakes are golden-brown at the edges. Cool on the tray then transfer the cakes to a wire rack.

Lime Curd Tarts

When, in the eighteenth century, the Royal Navy replaced the daily issue of lemons - given to sailors to prevent scurvy - with cheaper limes, English sailors were dubbed 'Limeys', a nickname which survived until not that long ago. These tarts have an attractive fresh citrus flavour.

Oven: 200°C/Fan 180°C/Gas 6 then 180°C/Fan 160°C/Gas 4 **Baking time:** 10-12 minutes
Makes: 18 tarts **Equipment:** 7.5cm (3in.) fluted pastry cutter, patty tins, buttered

Pastry:
175g (6oz) flour
30g (1oz) caster sugar
90g (3oz) butter, softened
1 egg yolk

Lime Curd Filling:
2 limes
2 large eggs
90g (3oz) caster sugar
60g (2oz) butter, softened or melted

Sieve the flour and sugar into a shallow mixing bowl or a cold work surface. Add the butter and egg yolk and use the fingertips to mix the ingredients together. Slide small handfuls of the mixture sideways until the dough easily forms a ball. Wrap the pastry in plastic and chill for 15 minutes. On a lightly floured board, roll out the pastry thinly and use the pastry cutter to make 18 circles to line the prepared patty tins. Prick the bases and chill for 15 minutes.

Bake the pastry cases blind in the preheated oven for 6-7 minutes until the pastry is set and is starting to change colour at the edge. Remove from the oven and lower the heat as above.

Meanwhile prepare the filling. Wash and dry the limes. Finely grate the zest into a bowl and add the strained juice. Beat in the eggs, sugar and butter. Spoon the filling into the pastry cases and bake for 5-6 minutes until the filling is set. Cool slightly, then carefully transfer the tarts from the patty tins to a wire rack.

Chocolate Coconut Squares

Simple to make and ideal for the school holidays. The mixture is baked in a shallow cake tin then topped with melted chocolate and cut into squares; the recipe is slightly adapted from the cookery book of the Cornmillers Guild.

Oven: 190°C/Fan 170°C/Gas 5 **Baking time:** 20-25 minutes **Makes:** 18 squares
Equipment: 30 x 18cm (12 x 7 in.) shallow cake tin, lined

230g (8oz) butter
120g (4oz) dark muscovado sugar
175g (6oz) whole-wheat flour
30g (1oz) cocoa
175g (6oz) desiccated coconut, unsweetened

Frosting:
200g (7oz) plain or milk chocolate
2-3 tablespoons milk
walnut size knob of butter
a little extra dessicated coconut

Cream the butter with the sugar until light and fluffy. Add the flour, cocoa and coconut and mix together to form a firm dough. If the flour is very dry you may need to add a little milk. Turn the dough into the prepared tin and smooth level with the back of a fork.

Bake in the preheated oven until just shrinking from the tin. Place the tin on a heatproof surface and leave to cool slightly. Break the chocolate into pieces and melt with the milk in a heatproof dish in a microwave oven. Remove from the oven and add the butter and stir gently until smooth. Spread the icing over the baked mixture while it is still hot and sprinkle over the extra coconut. Set aside until cold then cut into squares.

Hot Strawberry Tarts

As strawberries cook, they release their flavour and fragrance, filling the kitchen with a beguiling aroma. I've tried to capture such fruity attributes in these shallow tarts that are served straight from the oven.

Oven: 200°C/Fan 180°C/Gas 6 **Baking time:** 12-15 minutes **Makes:** 6 tarts
Equipment: 2 large non-stick baking sheets

250g (approx 8oz) prepared all-butter puff pastry
flour
1-2 tablespoons milk or cream
250g (8oz) ripe firm strawberries
100g (3½ oz) ripe raspberries
100g (3½ oz) caster sugar
30g (1oz) ground almonds
1 teaspoon cornflour

Cut the pastry dough into 6 equal pieces and shape each one into a ball. On a floured board, roll out the first piece quite thinly then cut round an upturned saucer about 14cm (5½ in.) across to make a circle. Use a fish slice to transfer the pastry disc to a baking sheet and use an upturned cup about 10.5cm (4 in.) across to mark a circle - do not cut through the pastry, leave a neat margin at the edge. Brush the margin with milk or cream. Repeat with the other pieces of pastry allowing a good space between each. If you wish, the pastry can now be covered with a cloth and stored in a cold place for 1-2 hours until needed.

Rinse the strawberries in cold water and drain well. Remove the stalks and cut each strawberry in half into a mixing bowl and add the rinsed raspberries. In a saucer mix 2 tablespoons of the caster sugar with the ground almonds. Stir the rest of the caster sugar with the cornflour into the fruit until well coated and the juice from the strawberries starts to dissolve the sugar.

Divide the almond mixture between the pastry discs, spreading it fairly evenly over the centres. Arrange the sugared fruit on top with the cut side facing down and the narrow ends of the strawberries towards the pastry margin, heaping slightly in the centre.

Bake the tarts in the preheated oven until the pastry edges are golden brown. Serve the tarts straight away with thick West Country cream.

Devon Blizzard Cake

One winter morning, we awoke to discover a blizzard had snowed us in. The roads were impassable, the schools were closed, and in my pottery a layer of powdery snow covered every unfired pot, destroying each one as it melted. I took to my warm kitchen and began baking. This popular cake has a layer of snowy meringue covering the chocolate ice cream earth, dotted with a few green shoots of pistachio nuts, sitting on a layer of chocolate sponge cake. In fact, it's my version of Baked Alaska. If the cake is for a celebration, I add a cake firework on top to provide a sparkling shower of light.

Oven: 180°C/Fan 160°C/Gas 4 **Baking time:** 25-30 minutes **Makes:** 16-20 portion cake
Equipment: 20cm (8 in.) spring-clip tin, buttered and base-lined

30g (1oz) cocoa powder
4 tablespoons hot water
120g (4oz) dark muscovado sugar
120g (4oz) butter, softened
2 eggs
120g (4oz) self-raising flour
1 litre (1¾ pt) chocolate ice cream
20 shelled pistachio nuts
3 egg whites
175g (6oz) caster sugar

Blend the cocoa with the hot water in a mixing bowl. Sieve the sugar into the bowl and add the butter, eggs and flour. Use an electric beater to mix for 1-2 minutes until smooth. Spoon the mixture into the prepared cake tin and smooth level.

Bake in the preheated oven until springy in the centre and just starting to shrink from the tin. Cool in the tin then unclip the side and remove. If you wish, the cake can be left on the metal base and frozen, wrapped in plastic, until needed.

To assemble the cake: spoon the ice cream on top of the cake making a high dome shape and add the pistachio nuts, pushing them into the ice cream. Return the cake to the freezer.

When ready to serve the cake, whisk the egg whites until stiff and gradually whisk in half the sugar and then the rest to make a stiff meringue. Spread the meringue over the ice cream and cake to make a swirly pattern to resemble a snow drift .

The meringue needs to be toasted a little to set it. Either do this with a chef's flame-torch, moving it quickly over the meringue to produce an attractive caramel colour in some places. Or place in a hot oven until the meringue has changed colour in some places. This happens quite suddenly and you need to remove the cake from the oven immediately before the meringue starts to burn. Place on a serving plate and serve straight away, cut into wedge-shaped slices.

Apple Sauce Cake

The apple sauce forms a moist layer in the middle of this spiced cake made with wholemeal flour and sultanas. An ideal cake for serving warm at breakfast or brunch with West Country honey or maple syrup.

Oven: 180°C/Fan 160°C/Gas 4 **Baking time:** 40-50 minutes **Makes:** 9 large or 16 small portion cake
Equipment: 18cm (7in.) square cake tin, lined

Apple Sauce:
450g (1lb) dessert apples such as Cox's Orange
2-3 tablepoons water
strip of lemon peel
60g (2oz) caster sugar or to taste
60g (2oz) sultanas
grated zest of ½ lemon

Cake:
175g (6oz) butter
175g (6oz) light soft brown sugar
3 eggs
90g (3oz) self-raising flour
175g (6oz) self-raising wholemeal flour
½ teaspoon mixed spice or ground cinnamon
1 tablespoon demerara sugar

Peel and core the apples and chop into pieces. Cook with the water, the lemon peel and half the sugar over a medium heat until soft enough to mash into a puree which need not be completely smooth. Discard the lemon peel and measure the puree in a jug, it should be close to 425ml (15fl oz) Stir in the rest of the sugar, the sultanas and the zest of lemon and allow to cool.

Cream the butter with the sugar until fluffy. Beat in the eggs separately then stir in both kinds of flour and the spice. Spoon a little over half the mixture into the prepared tin and smooth level. Spread the apple sauce over the top, cover with the rest of the cake mixture and sprinkle with the demerara sugar.

Bake in the preheated oven until the cake is golden brown and just shrinking from the sides of the tin. Cool for a few minutes then transfer the cake to a level board or plate, cut into portions and serve.

Plymtree Harvest Cake

Ever since I published my mother's recipe in *Cake Stall*, readers have written to tell me that this good, simple fruit cake has become such a firm favourite that it is now baked and appreciated in many other countries too.

Oven: 160°C/Fan 140°C/Gas 3 **Baking time:** 1½-1¾ hours **Makes:** 16 portion cake
Equipment: 20 cm (8 in.) round or square tin - buttered and lined

230g (8oz) butter, softened
230g (8oz) caster or light muscovado sugar
4 eggs
350g (12oz) plain flour
1 teaspoon baking powder
450g (1lb) mixed dried fruit - seedless raisins, sultanas, currants
120g (4oz) dried or glacé cherries, quartered
60g (2oz) candied peel, chopped

Measure the ingredients into a warmed mixing bowl and stir well until you have a stiff mixture. That's all there is to it. Spoon the mixture into the prepared cake tin and smooth level.

Bake in the preheated oven until the cake is cooked, when it will be slightly firm to the touch and a slim bamboo skewer comes out clean from the centre. Cool in the tin for 45 minutes then turn on to a wire rack to cool. When cold, wrap in greaseproof paper and keep in an air-tight plastic container in a cold place until needed. The cake keeps well, in the fridge or the freezer, for 2-3 weeks.

Variation: add ½ tsp mixed spice to the mixture and sprinkle halved or slivered blanched almonds over the top of the cake before baking.

Devon Apple Butter

A traditional version of apple jam, subtly spiced and specially good on buttered toast and freshly baked bread - an ideal way of utilising windfall fruit.

2.25kg (5lb) eating apples and/or crab apples
1 litre (1¾ pt) water or 50/50 cider and water
granulated or caster sugar
1 teaspoon ground cinnamon
1 teaspoon ground cloves

Wash and drain the apples then cut into quarters discarding any bruised or damaged fruit. In a large pan simmer the apples with the water or cider mixture over moderate heat until cooked and soft enough to mash.

Working in batches, press the apple mixture through a moderately fine sieve to produce a puree and discard the debris in the sieve. Measure the puree, and for every 500g (1lb) allow 350g (12oz) of sugar. Return the puree to the pan and cook, stirring all the time, until thick enough to leave a clean line when a wooden spoon is drawn across the base of the pan.

Stir in the sugar until dissolved then bring to the boil. Add the spices and cook, stirring now and then, until the mixture is thick enough to leave the sides of the pan. Spoon the apple butter into small hot jars, seal tightly and label then store in a cold place until needed.

Somerset

Last autumn, as the train crossed the county boundary into Somerset, I glimpsed a group of South American llamas grazing in an apple orchard; a measure perhaps of how much has now changed in this lovely county that stretches from Bath to Taunton.

Much of Somerset lies at sea level, the Mendip Hills to the East and the Quantocks in the West seem to contain the low lying fertile soil of the 'levels'. It is dotted with ancient apple orchards and standing almost like a centre pin is Glastonbury and its Tor, famous for its music festival and mythical associations. It is an ancient and diverse region containing evidence of man's earliest activities, preserved in the famous peat bogs, as well as the outstanding geology of Cheddar's caves.

It has, for many centuries, been identified with two principal foods - cider and cheese. The moist climate, with warm summers, favours both apple orchards and grazing meadowland. Today Cheddar cheese has achieved worldwide fame and recognised status in the European Union and cider making continues to develop thanks to the ingenuity and skill of pioneering individuals and local artisans.

One example of this local initiative is the work of Julian Temperley whose aged cider brandy is similar to Normandy's calvados. This highly esteemed spirit is used in my kitchen as a delicious addition to enhance the flavour of cakes, syllabubs and other Somerset-inspired dishes; and cider appears frequently in old recipes such as Devon Cider Cake and Somerset Cider Fruit Cake. Not only does the bubbling liquid aerate a mixture in a similar way to bicarbonate of soda, but cider also contributes a pleasing taste to a cake. Dried fruit such as raisins, sultanas and currants, steeped in cider overnight before making a fruit cake, impart an excellent flavour to the baked result. For centuries, cider was made on the farm, and I vividly remember watching my neighbour perform this autumn ritual in the cider house built to one side of his yard. Dominating this space was an enormous oak cider press, whose wide hand-carved screw would be slowly turned by a group of local men, as they compressed the layers of crushed apples known as the cheese. Each layer of apples was sandwiched between thick straw mats that strained the juice before it ran into a stone trough. Wooden barrels and kegs of fresh apple juice ferment quite quickly when stored in the cider house so as soon as possible the cloudy liquid would be poured into jugs. The result was a thirst-quenching beverage known as scrumpy ... and notoriously deceptive in its alcoholic punch!

'Oh! who can ever be tired of Bath,' wrote Jane Austen in Northanger Abbey. The social activities of Bath stand in sharp contrast to the hard physical work of the farm but thanks to the many writers who have lived there, we know a great deal about the food and baking of this stylish city. The Pump Room was a lively social centre in Regency times when fashionable ladies partook of a little light refreshment such as gingerbread valentines, shortbread biscuits and tiny meringues. A few streets away in her cellar kitchen - now a museum - Sally Lunn baked the famous brioche-like teacake named after her. Other bakers produced Bath Buns and the still-popular biscuits known as Bath Olivers.

Today's visitors to Bath, no longer arriving by horse-drawn transport, can choose from a large number of cafes, coffee shops, and restaurants. These make for a ready supply of comforting and nourishing resting places to pause for a while and consider the pleasures of Somerset.

Recipes for Somerset

86 Sally Lunn Teacakes
88 Apple and Cheddar Cheese Scone Ring
89 Bath Buns
90 Somerset Raisin Glory
92 Sedgemoor Easter Cake
93 Spiced Apple Cake with Apple Brandy Cream
94 Ripe Raspberry Roll
96 Lavender and Orange Cake
97 Cider Fruit Cake
98 Pear and Perry Cake
100 Frosted Yoghurt Cake
102 Somerset Mincemeat Pies
104 Somerset Mincemeat
105 Toffee Apples
106 Gingerbread Valentines
108 Japonais Cakes
109 Eleventh Hour Kisses
110 Walnut Meringues filled with Coffee Cream
111 Digestive Biscuits
112 Dark Chocolate Brandy Mousse Cake
114 Boiled Fruit Cake
115 Bath Teashop Brownies

Sally Lunn Teacakes

'Now for the tea of our host
Now for the rollicking bun
Now for the muffin and toast
And now for the gay Sally Lunn.'

'The Sorcerer', Gilbert and Sullivan.

Both Mrs Agnes Leyel and Florence White write that Sally Lunn teacakes were a Good Friday speciality in Regency Bath, and that they should be served warm with clotted cream. Excellent advice, though when I last sampled these light brioche-like cakes in the Sally Lunn tea room, each half was served freshly toasted with a choice of melted chocolate or what tasted like cream cheese blended with sugar and plenty of ground cinnamon.

Oven: 200°C/Fan 180°C/Gas 6 **Baking time:** approximately 20 minutes **Makes:** 3 teacakes
Equipment: three 10-12cm (4-5 in.) diameter cake tins, greased

350g (12oz) white bread flour
1½ teaspoons rapid-rise dried yeast
60g (2oz) butter
175ml (6fl oz) milk
1 tablespoon caster sugar
½ teaspoon salt
1 egg, beaten
½ lemon, grated zest

Glaze:
1 tablespoon milk
1 tablespoon caster sugar

Measure the flour and yeast into a mixing bowl. Melt the butter in a small pan then stir in the milk, sugar and salt until the mixture is luke warm. Pour onto the flour with the beaten egg and the lemon zest and mix well using a wooden spoon for 3-4 minutes or with an electric beater fitted with a dough hook until the mixture feels elastic.

Cover the bowl with a roomy plastic bag and leave in a warm place for about 1 hour or until the dough has doubled in size. Beat the dough for 1 minute then divide between the prepared tins. Leave in a warm place for 20-30 minutes until the dough is puffy.

Bake in the preheated oven for about 20 minutes or until the teacakes are golden then remove from the oven. Stir together the milk and sugar to make a glaze and brush over the tops of the teacakes. Serve the Sally Lunn cakes while still warm.

Apple And Cheddar Cheese Scone Ring

Fresh herbs and a local cheese make these scones ideal picnic food or to accompany a soup or salad.

Oven: 200°C/Fan 180°C/Gas 6 **Baking time:** 15-17 minutes **Makes:** 2 small or 1 large scone ring
Equipment: 5cm (2in.) fluted pastry cutter, baking sheet, lightly floured

120g (4oz) self-raising flour
120g (4oz) self-raising wholemeal flour
1 teaspoon baking powder
¼ teaspoon salt
60g (2oz) butter
2 medium dessert apples, cored and finely grated
2 tablespoons chopped fresh herbs - chives, oregano, rosemary, sage
60g (2oz) Cheddar or other West Country cheese, grated
1 egg mixed with milk to make 150ml (5fl oz)
a little extra milk

In a mixing bowl stir all the flour with the baking powder. Cut then rub in the butter until the mixture resembles breadcrumbs. Stir in the grated apple and almost all the herbs and grated cheese, reserving some of each for the tops of the scones, and mix in the egg liquid to form a soft dough.

Turn the dough on to a floured board and gently knead for one minute. Roll out until 1cm (½in.) thick and use the pastry cutter to cut out 14 scones. Arrange the scones, their sides touching, in one or two circles on the prepared baking sheet. Brush the tops of the scones with the extra milk and sprinkle over the reserved chopped herbs and grated cheese.

Bake towards the top of the preheated oven until well-risen and golden-brown. Cool slightly then transfer to a wire rack or a cloth-lined basket for serving warm.

Bath Buns

Just as Chelsea Buns originated in London, so Bath Buns decorated with crushed sugar hail from the Somerset spa town on the banks of the river Avon. A recipe from the 18th century reveals that Bath Buns were once far richer and included sherry, rosewater, caraway comfits, eggs and butter. Today's more restrained recipe comes from the Somerset Women's Institute.

Oven: 220°C/Fan 200°C/Gas 7 **Baking time:** 10 minutes **Makes:** 8-12 buns
Equipment: baking sheet, greased

300g (10oz) white bread flour
90g (3oz) butter or lard
1½ teaspoon rapid-rise dried yeast
150ml (5fl oz) lukewarm milk
1 egg, beaten
90g (3oz) caster sugar
90g (3oz) sultanas
60g (2oz) candied peel, chopped
1 tablespoon milk
30g (1oz) white sugar cubes

Measure the flour into a mixing bowl and rub in the butter or lard until the mixture resembles breadcrumbs. Stir in the yeast and pour in the lukewarm milk and the beaten egg. Use a wooden spoon to mix until well combined then beat for 1-2 minutes until the dough starts to feel elastic. Scrape down the dough and cover the bowl with a roomy plastic bag. Set aside in a warm place for 1 hour or until the dough has doubled in size.

Mix the sugar, sultanas and chopped peel into the dough and beat well. Take a rounded tablespoon of the dough and form into a ball. Place on the prepared baking sheet and repeat with the rest of the dough. Brush the tops of the buns with milk. Crush the cube sugar in a plastic bag to produce sugar nibs and sprinkle the sugar over the tops of the buns.

Bake in the preheated oven until golden brown. Cool on the tray for 10 minutes then serve or allow to cool on a wire rack.

Somerset Raisin Glory

Cheddar cheese blended with raisins, lemon juice and ground almonds is an unusual combination of flavours for a filled pastry with its echoes of the more familiar mince pie.

Oven: 180°C/Fan 160°C/Gas 4 **Baking time:** 40 minutes **Makes:** 16 pieces
Equipment: 23cm (9 in.) square shallow cake tin, base-lined

Pastry:
350g (12oz) flour
200g (7oz) butter
6-7 tablespoons milk

Filling:
230g (8oz) seedless raisins
boiling water
1 lemon
120g (4oz) caster sugar
120g (4oz) ground almonds
¼ teaspoon ground cinnamon
good pinch of ground mace
230g (8oz) mild Cheddar cheese, grated
grated nutmeg
1 tablespoon milk
1 tablespoon granulated sugar

To make the pastry, measure the flour into a bowl, add the butter cut in pieces and rub in until the mixture resembles breadcrumbs. Add enough milk to mix to a dough then shape into a ball and leave on a floured board under the upturned bowl while you prepare the filling.

Measure the raisins into a bowl and cover with boiling water. Drain well and return to the bowl. Stir in the finely grated zest and juice of the lemon with the sugar, ground almonds, cinnamon, mace and grated cheese.

Divide the pastry and roll out half to fit into the base of the cake tin allowing it to come up the sides a little. Spoon the raisin filling on to the pastry spreading it level and grate nutmeg over the top. Roll out the rest of the pastry and press down lightly over the filling. Brush with milk and sprinkle over the granulated sugar. Use a knife to mark the pastry into 16 squares taking care not to cut all the way through.

Bake in the preheated oven until the pastry is baked to golden brown. Cool before cutting into squares and serving, if you wish, with cream.

Sedgemoor Easter Cake

A traditional Somerset flat cake, sweetly spiced and speckled with currants, and which in 1931 starred at the first exhibition of the English Folk Cookery Association. The redoubtable Florence White founded the association and compiled 'Good Things in England' - an unrivalled 'gastronomic map' of 853 recipes from across the country. The recipe for this Easter cake advises making small cakes but I prefer to bake one large teacake and serve it straight from the oven with plenty of coffee at a late breakfast or mid-morning during the Easter holiday.

Oven: 190°C/Fan 170°C/Gas 5 **Baking time:** 20 minutes **Makes:** 6-8 portion teacake
Equipment: baking sheet, greased

230g (8oz) flour
120g (4oz) butter
120g (4oz) caster sugar
120g (4oz) currants
½ teaspoon ground cinnamon
½ teaspoon mixed spice
1 egg
2 tablespoons brandy or cider

Sift the flour into a bowl and add the butter in small pieces then rub in until the mixture resembles breadcrumbs. Stir in the sugar, currants and spices. Beat the egg with the brandy or cider and add to the bowl. Mix to a soft dough and shape into a ball. Roll out the dough on a lightly floured surface until 1cm (½ in.) thick and use a fish slice to transfer to the prepared baking sheet.

Bake in the preheated oven until golden brown. Use a fish slice to move the teacake to a wooden platter and cut into 6 or 8 portions. Serve while still hot.

Spiced Apple Cake With Apple Brandy Cream

Though originally from Holland, this attractive apple cake is often baked in the West Country using local apples. Serve the cake straight from the oven with the cream.

Oven: 200°C/Fan 180°C/Gas 6 **Baking time:** 35-40 minutes **Makes:** 12-16 pieces
Equipment: 20cm (8in.) square shallow cake tin, lined

90g (3oz) butter
150g (5oz) light muscovado sugar
½ teaspoon ground cinnamon
¼ teaspoon grated nutmeg
3-4 medium dessert West Country apples, peeled and sliced
½ orange, finely grated zest
1 egg mixed with milk to make 150ml (5fl oz)
175g (6oz) self-raising flour

Apple Brandy Cream:
300ml (10fl oz) double cream
1 tablespoon caster sugar
3-4 teaspoons Somerset Apple Brandy or French Calvados (optional)

Melt 30g (1 oz) of the butter in a small pan and keep warm. Measure 60g (2oz) of the sugar into a roomy plastic bag, add the spices and shake together. Add the sliced apple and shake again until coated with the spiced sugar.

Slightly warm the remaining butter in a mixing bowl until softened, add the remaining sugar and grated orange zest and beat together until light and creamy. Gradually mix in the egg/milk liquid alternately with the flour until well combined. Spoon the mixture into the cake tin and smooth level. Brush with the melted butter and arrange the apple slices in rows on top. Sprinkle any spiced sugar left in the bag over the apples.

Bake in the preheated oven until a wooden skewer comes out clean from the centre. Meanwhile whisk the cream until thick but still glossy. Gently mix in the sugar and the brandy. Spoon the cream into a bowl and serve with the cake.

Ripe Raspberry Roll

An attractive, rolled sponge cake filled with West Country cream and ripe raspberries and ideal for a summer birthday or celebration.

Oven: 200°C/Fan 180°C/Gas 6 **Baking time:** 12-15 minutes **Makes:** 10 portion cake
Equipment: 32.5 x 23cm (13 x 9 in.) Swiss roll tin, lined; clean tea cloth

3 eggs
few drops of vanilla essence
90g (3oz) caster sugar
90g (3oz) flour
¼ teaspoon baking powder
a little extra caster sugar

Filling:
4 rounded tablespoons raspberry jam
300ml (10fl oz) double cream
4 tablespoons milk
1-2 tablespoons caster sugar
300g (10oz) ripe raspberries
1 teaspoon icing sugar (optional)

Whisk the eggs with the vanilla essence and sugar, in an electric mixer or in a bowl set over simmering water using a hand-held electric beater, until the mixture is pale and foamy and the whisk leaves a trail over the surface. Tip the flour and baking powder into a fine sieve, dust a layer over the top and gently fold in the flour with a balloon whisk retaining as much air as possible. Repeat until all the flour has been incorporated then pour the mixture into the prepared cake tin and spread evenly.

Bake in the preheated oven until the cake is springy to the touch in the centre. Cool in the tin for 2 minutes then turn out on to the tea-cloth sprinkled with the extra caster sugar. Peel off the lining paper and carefully roll up the cake from the short side, allowing the cloth to take the place of the filling, and leave wrapped in the cloth while you prepare the fruit and cream.

Sieve the raspberry jam into a basin and discard the seeds. Whisk the cream with the milk and sugar until thick and glossy. Unroll the cake and brush the surface with the sieved jam. Spread the cream on top but leave 2-3 tablespoons of cream in the bowl for decorating the cake. Reserve 10 perfect raspberries for decoration and scatter the rest over the layer of cream then use the back of a spoon to push them into it. Now carefully re-roll the cake so that the end is underneath and transfer it to a serving plate. Use the reserved cream to arrange 10 teaspoons of cream in a row along the top of the cake and place a raspberry in the centre of each. Serve the cake straight away or refrigerate until ready to serve.

Lavender And Orange Cake

A marriage of citrus and lavender flavours works well in an almond-rich cake decorated with trails of glace icing.

Oven: 180°C/Fan 160°C/Gas 4 **Baking time:** 30-35 minutes **Makes:** 8 portion cake
Equipment: 20cm (8in.) spring-clip tin, buttered and base-lined

120g (4oz)butter
90g (3oz) caster sugar
2 eggs
½ orange
1 teaspoon fresh or dried lavender flowers
60g (2oz) self-raising flour
90g (3oz) ground almonds

Icing:
120g (4oz) icing sugar
few extra lavender flowers

Cream the butter with the caster sugar until light and fluffy. Beat in the eggs separately with the grated zest of orange and the lavender flowers. Fold in the sieved flour and the ground almonds. Spoon into the prepared cake tin and smooth level.

Bake in the preheated oven until the cake is cooked and just beginning to shrink from the tin. Cool in the tin for 10 minutes then release the sides and slide the cake on its paper onto a wire rack.

Make the icing by sieving the icing sugar into a bowl. Stir in sufficient strained orange juice to make a pouring consistency. Take a dessertspoon of icing and trickle it across the top of the cake in fine lines. Repeat until the cake is covered, sprinkle over the extra lavender flowers and set the cake aside for an hour or until the icing has set. For the best flavour serve the cake the same day.

Cider Fruit Cake

Dried fruit soaked in West Country cider for a few hours imparts an excellent flavour to this cake.

Oven: 180°C/Fan 160°C/Gas 4 **Baking time:** 60-70 minutes **Makes:** 8-12 portion cake
Equipment: 20cm (8 in.) cake tin, buttered and base-lined

265g (9oz) mixed dried fruit – seedless raisins, sultanas and currants
4 tablespoons sweet or dry cider
175g (6oz) butter
175g (6oz) light muscovado sugar
3 eggs
265g (9oz) self-raising flour
1 teaspoon mixed sweet spice

Measure the fruit into a bowl, pour over the cider and leave overnight or until the liquid has been absorbed by the fruit. If need be, this stage can be speeded up by warming the fruit and cider in a pan over low heat, but cool the mixture before adding to the other ingredients.

Cream the butter with the sugar until pale and fluffy. Add the eggs, one at a time, beating each in well with a little flour to prevent the mixture from separating. Sift in the rest of the flour with the mixed spice, folding this into the mixture alternately with the cider-soaked fruit. Spoon into the prepared cake tin and smooth level.

Bake in the preheated oven until a slim bamboo skewer comes out clean from the centre of the cake. Cool in the tin for 10 minutes then turn out on to a wire rack.

Pear And Perry Cake

Perry resembles cider but is made with pears instead of apples. Many of the old varieties of perry pears have disappeared but some dedicated growers - 'You plant pears for your heirs' is a West Country saying - have replanted former orchards with this once highly-valued fruit. Perry adds a lovely flavour to this cake with its slices of pear, scattered with toasted almonds, spiralling out from the centre like the spokes of a wheel. Serve the cake warm with plain yoghurt or thick cream.

Oven: 180°C/Fan 160°C/Gas 4 **Baking time:** 45-50 minutes **Makes:** 8 portion cake
Equipment: 20cm (8in.) spring-clip tin, buttered and base-lined

2 medium-size ripe Williams or Conference pears
2 tablespoons Somerset Perry
1 tablespoon clear honey
100g (3½ oz) butter
100g (3½ oz) caster sugar
¼ lemon, finely grated zest
2 eggs
100g (3½ oz) ground almonds
60g (2oz) self-raising flour
15g (½ oz) flaked almonds, lightly toasted

Wash and dry the pears - Conference pears should be peeled, thin-skinned Williams pears can stay as they are - then quarter and core them. Divide each pear quarter lengthways to give 16 pear slices in all and place them in a single layer on a plate. Mix the perry with the honey and spoon over the slices.

Make the cake by creaming the butter with the sugar and lemon zest until light and fluffy. Beat in the eggs separately. Mix in the ground almonds and flour. In the base of the cake tin, arrange the pear slices with the slices radiating out from centre. Scatter the flaked almonds in the gaps between the pear slices. Carefully place spoonfuls of cake mixture on top, taking care not to dislodge the fruit, and smooth level with the back of the spoon. Set aside the remaining perry mixture in the dish.

Bake the cake in the preheated oven until the cake is cooked and is just starting to shrink from the tin, and a slim bamboo skewer comes out clean from the centre. Cool in the tin for 5 minutes then unclip and remove the side of the tin, turn the cake upside down onto a wire rack or flat serving dish and carefully peel off the baking paper. Drizzle the reserved perry over the cake and serve the cake warm.

Frosted Yoghurt Cake

Years ago, when I wrote cookery articles for the Exeter Express & Echo newspaper, kind readers sent me recipes, useful information and even samples of their cooking. One morning, a tub of home-made yoghurt arrived from a farmer's wife in East Devon which I used as a starter for my own supply for some months. Since then, more dairy farmers in the south-west, notably in Somerset, have started to make excellent yoghurt. Plain, whole-milk yoghurt is best for this simple cake with its subtle flavour.

Oven: 180°C/Fan 160°C/Gas 4 **Baking time:** 40-50 minutes **Makes:** 16-20 portion cake
Equipment: 18cm (7in.) square loose-bottomed cake tin, lined

4 eggs, separated
125ml (4fl oz) plain natural yoghurt
125ml (4fl oz) sunflower oil
½ teaspoon vanilla essence
½ teaspoon grated zest of lemon or orange
230g (8oz) caster sugar
270g (9oz) flour
1 teaspoon baking powder

Frosting:
175g (6oz) icing sugar
2-3 tablespoons plain yoghurt
1-2 drops vanilla essence
few strands of lemon or orange zest

In a mixing bowl, stir the egg yolks with the yoghurt, sunflower oil, vanilla essence, lemon zest and sugar. Stir in the flour sifted with the baking powder. In another bowl whisk the egg whites until stiff and gently fold into the mixture. Pour the mixture into the prepared tin and smooth level.

Bake in the preheated oven until cake is risen and golden brown and when a slim bamboo skewer comes out clean from the centre. Cool the cake in the tin for 5 minutes then transfer to a wire rack to cool.

Make the frosting by sifting the icing sugar into a bowl and gradually blend in the yoghurt, a little at a time until the frosting is spreadable. Mix in the vanilla essence and spread the frosting over the cake leaving a pattern of swirls. Sprinkle the strands of lemon or orange zest on top. Set the cake aside for 1 hour or until the frosting has set.

Somerset Mincemeat Pies

Home-made mince pies are a part of traditional Christmas festivities. If you cut out a star shape from the pastry lids before covering the mincemeat and baking, it is easy to add a splash of festive spirit to the hot pies by trickling rum or brandy into them just before serving.

Oven: 200°C/Fan 180°C/Gas 6 **Baking time:** 20 minutes **Makes:** 12 pies
Equipment: 7.5 cm (3 in.) and 6.5 cm (2½ in.) fluted pastry cutters, patty tin - buttered

Sweet Shortcrust Pastry:
230g (8oz) flour
30g (1oz) icing sugar
135 g (4½ oz) butter
½ lemon or orange, grated zest
4 tablespoons milk

Filling:
230g (8oz) Somerset mincemeat (p104)
a little extra milk
1 -2 tablespoons granulated sugar

Sift the flour and sugar into a bowl, cut and rub in the butter with the grated citrus zest until the mixture resembles breadcrumbs. Mix to a soft dough with the milk and shape it into a ball.
If you have time, rest the pastry under an upturned bowl or chill it, wrapped, in the fridge for 30 minutes to make the dough easier to handle.

On a floured board, roll out just over half the pastry to 3mm (⅛ in.) thickness. With the larger pastry cutter, cut out 12 discs of pastry and line the patty tins. Place one rounded dessertspoon of mincemeat in each pastry case.

Roll out the remaining pastry and use the smaller cutter to cut out another 12 discs for the lids cut out a star shape from each if you wish. Brush milk over the underside of each lid and place over the mincemeat, making sure it's central. Press down gently at the edge to join the two pastry layers. Brush each pie with milk and sprinkle with sugar.

Bake in the preheated oven until the pastry is golden brown. Cool in the patty tin for 10 minutes then serve immediately or transfer the pies to a wire rack.

Somerset Mincemeat

The first edition of Mrs Beeton's tome on Household Management (1861), includes a recipe for mincemeat containing minced lean beef - a long-established style that is now rarely seen in Britain. Yet, in Frome in 1852 - according to Florence White - cooks were already in the vanguard of food fashion by favouring a modern preference for this excellent, lighter, meat-free version.

Makes: approximately 2kg (4lb) mincemeat

2 large lemons
450g (1lb) dark muscovado sugar
230g (8oz) currants
230g (8oz) muscatel raisins, seeded and chopped, or seedless raisins
230g (8oz) sultanas
230g (8oz) candied peel, chopped
230g (8oz) almonds, blanched and slivered
230g (8oz) butter, melted or grated suet
½ teaspoon ground cinnamon
½ teaspoon ground cloves
½ teaspoon grated nutmeg
¼ teaspoon ground mace
150ml (5fl oz) brandy or sherry

Wash the lemons and cut in half, squeeze out the juice and set aside. Boil the halved lemons in water to cover until the peel is tender then discard the liquid. Use scissors to cut the lemon peel into pieces and puree in a processor. Scoop the lemon puree into a mixing bowl and stir in the rest of the ingredients with the strained lemon juice. Taste to check that the balance of flavours is to your liking - extra sugar or spice may be called for.

This mincemeat may be used straight away or can be stored in sterilised, air-tight jars in a cool, dark place until required.

Toffee Apples

November the Fifth is celebrated with tremendous gusto in many parts of the West Country. Ottery St Mary has a tradition of carrying tar barrels of flames through the town and many villages have a communal bonfire with a straw-filled Guy Fawkes and a firework display. Toffee apples with wooden handles are part of the fun.

Makes: 8 toffee apples

8 small eating apples
8 short strong wooden skewers
450g (1lb) granulated or caster sugar
8 tablespoons water

Wash and dry the apples. Remove the stalks and fix a wooden skewer into the stalk end of each fruit to make the handle.

Dissolve the sugar in the water in a heavy-based pan over low heat, stirring all the time. Raise the heat and boil until the syrup is golden-brown and reaches 135°C or small crack stage on a sugar thermometer. Immediately remove the toffee from the heat because if allowed to cook until dark brown the taste can be bitter.

Holding an apple by its handle, dip it into the liquid toffee and gently turn until the whole fruit is coated. Place the toffee apple - handle in the air - on baking parchment.
Repeat with the other apples and leave to cool and the toffee has set. Eat the toffee apples within a few hours, otherwise wrap each one in cellophane to prevent the toffee from softening.

Gingerbread Valentines

Shaped and moulded, highly-spiced gingerbread was a Georgian speciality. In Cakes of England, Mrs Leyel writes: 'Bath was then the centre of the fashionable world and not only Gingerbread Valentines, but Sally Lunns originated there.' When stored in an air-tight container, these heart-shaped biscuits are very crisp and perfect for dipping - briefly, a little at a time - into a cup of tea which will reveal their rich spicy flavour. To soften the gingerbread, simply leave the biscuits in the open air for a few hours before serving.

Oven: 180°C/Fan 160°C/Gas 4 **Baking time:** 12 -15 minutes **Makes:** 20-30 biscuits
Equipment: baking sheets, buttered, heart-shaped biscuit cutters - various sizes

60g (2oz) butter
60g (2oz) dark muscovado sugar
175g (6oz) golden syrup
230g (8oz) self-raising flour
¾ teaspoon ground ginger
½ teaspoon ground cinnamon
¼ teaspoon ground cloves
¼ teaspoon ground mace
good pinch ground allspice
60g (2oz) candied orange peel, very finely chopped

Melt the butter in a saucepan large enough for making the gingerbread mixture and remove from the heat. Measure the sugar and leave in the scale pan while you pour the syrup on top - remembering the total weight of both ingredients - then tip both into the saucepan and stir well. Mix in the flour sieved with the spices and add the candied peel. Stir well until you have a stiff dough which forms a ball. I usually divide the dough and roll out each half separately.

On a floured board roll out a ball of dough until 5mm (¼ in.) thick. Use a heart-shape cutter to make as many biscuits as possible. Re-roll the trimmings and cut out more biscuits, using a smaller size cutter if you have it. Arrange the biscuits, allowing space for expansion, on the prepared baking sheets.

Bake in the preheated oven until the biscuits are a deep amber colour. Try not to bake the biscuits too long or the colour will deepen and the flavour will be spoiled. Cool the biscuits on the baking sheet for 10 minutes then carefully transfer them, with a palette knife, to a wire rack.

The gingerbread biscuits are lovely served plain but sometimes I decorate them with piped white icing or by trailing diagonal lines across them in melted chocolate.

Japonais Cakes

Crisp, hazelnut meringues with a soft interior and sandwiched with coffee butter icing - another treat from a West Country teashop.

Oven: 160°C/Fan 140°C/Gas 3 **Baking time:** 25-30 minutes **Makes:** 12 cakes
Equipment: baking sheets - lined

2 egg whites
120g (4oz) caster sugar
1 tablespoons cornflour
60g (2oz) ground hazelnuts

Butter Icing:
120g (4oz) icing sugar
90g (3oz) butter
coffee essence to flavour
60g (2oz) melted chocolate (optional)

Whisk the egg whites until stiff. Sprinkle half the sugar over the meringue and whisk in. Sift the rest of the sugar with the cornflour and fold into the mixture with the ground hazelnuts until combined. Place dessertspoons of the mixture, well spaced, on the prepared baking sheets, allowing 12 on each.

Bake in the preheated oven until just changing colour at the edges. Cool on the baking sheet for 5 minutes then use a palette knife to carefully transfer the cakes to a wire rack.

Make the butter icing by sifting the icing sugar into a bowl, add the butter and blend together until smooth. Flavour to taste with coffee essence, adding a few drops at a time. Sandwich the cakes with the butter icing. Melted chocolate can be trickled over the top of each cake, if desired. Serve the cakes within an hour or so, before the meringue softens - otherwise freeze the cakes in an air-tight container until required.

Eleventh Hour Kisses

Biscuits known as kisses are said to be associated with English village life. The name is hardly heard these days but these macaroon-like biscuits are worth reviving. Serve the kisses singly or sandwiched with whipped cream.

Oven: 150°C/Fan 130°C/Gas 2 **Baking time:** 25-30 minutes **Makes:** 24 single biscuits
Equipment: 2 baking sheets - lined

2 egg whites
120g (4oz) caster sugar
90g (3oz) ground almonds
120g (4oz) dried apricots, finely chopped
1 tablespoon caster sugar

Whisk the egg whites until stiff. Spoon in half the sugar and whisk again then fold in the remaining sugar. Gently fold in the ground almonds and chopped apricots. Place dessertspoons of the mixture on the prepared baking sheets and sprinkle with the extra caster sugar.

Bake in the preheated oven until the biscuits are pale gold. Cool on the baking sheet for 5 minutes then transfer to a wire rack.

Walnut Meringues Filled With Coffee Cream

Oven: 100°C/Fan 90°C/Gas ¼ **Baking time:** 2-3 hours **Makes:** 14 small or 6 large, sandwiched meringues **Equipment:** 2 baking sheets, lined

60g (2oz) broken walnuts
60g (2oz) caster sugar
60g (2oz) light soft brown sugar
1 tablespoon cornflour
good pinch ground cinnamon
2 egg whites

Coffee Cream:
150ml (5fl oz) double cream
1 tablespoon caster sugar
½ teaspoon liquid coffee essence
1 teaspoon icing sugar

Toast the walnuts under a hot grill for a few minutes until starting to change colour. Cool then chop coarsely with a long-bladed knife on a wooden board. Sieve both kinds of sugar with the cornflour and cinnamon on to plate.

Whisk the egg whites until stiff and do not slide across the bowl when you tilt it. Gradually whisk in half the sugar mixture and fold in the rest with the walnuts. Use a teaspoon to place 28 small meringues, or a tablespoon to make 12 large ones, on the baking sheets leaving room for the mixture to spread.

Bake in the preheated oven until the meringues are crisp and no longer stick to the baking paper. Allow the meringues to cool in the oven. Then transfer to a wire rack or pack into a lidded plastic box and freeze until needed.

Whisk the cream until thick but still glossy and stir in the sugar and coffee essence. Sandwich each pair of meringues with the cream. Dust lightly with icing sugar and serve within 2 hours.

Digestive Biscuits

Home-made digestive biscuits are delicious, especially if made with locally-milled flour. The biscuits can be left plain or partly dipped in chocolate.

Oven: 180°C/Fan 160°C/Gas 4 **Baking time:** 15-20 minutes **Makes:** about 20 biscuits
Equipment: 6.5cm (2½ in.) plain or fluted pastry cutter, baking sheet, buttered

230g (8oz) whole wheat flour
30g (1oz) dark muscovado sugar
¼ teaspoon bicarbonate of soda
90g (3oz) butter
1 egg yolk or half a beaten egg
3 tablespoons milk
120g (4oz) plain dessert chocolate, melted (optional)

Measure the flour into a mixing bowl. Stir in the sugar sieved with the bicarbonate of soda and add the butter in pieces, then rub in with your fingertips. Mix the egg with the milk and stir into the dry ingredients to make a soft dough. Turn out on to a lightly floured work surface and roll out thinly until about 3 mm (⅛in.) thick. Use the pastry cutter to cut out the biscuits, then place them on the prepared baking sheet.

Dark Chocolate Brandy Mousse Cake

A good party cake: simple to make with no baking required and may be frozen until ready to serve. The dark chocolate mousse is layered with brandy and coffee-soaked sponge finger biscuits arranged in a loaf tin. I prefer to cut the cake into slices while it is frozen but for the best flavour allow the mousse to soften slightly in a fridge before serving. If you wish, the ground almonds in the recipe can be replaced with crumbs of crushed sponge fingers.

Makes: 14-16 portion cake **Equipment:** 1.2l (2pt) loaf tin, measuring 25 x 11x 7.5cm (10 x 4 x 3 in.), lightly buttered and lined with food film

300g (10 oz) plain 70% chocolate
500ml (18fl oz) whipping cream
60g (2oz) ground almonds
3-4 tablespoons caster sugar or to taste
150ml (5fl oz) strong black coffee
4 tablespoons brandy or armagnac
1 tablespoon caster sugar
30 sponge fingers
30g (1oz) flaked almonds, toasted

Break the chocolate into pieces and melt in a heatproof bowl in a microwave or over hot water. Gently stir the chocolate until smooth, then stand the bowl in shallow cold water until cool. Whisk the cream in a mixing bowl until thick and forming soft peaks. Gradually fold the chocolate into the cream with the sugar and the sieved ground almonds.

Spoon a layer of chocolate cream over the base of the prepared cake tin. Pour the coffee and brandy into a shallow dish and stir in the sugar. Dip the non-sugared side of a biscuit into the coffee mixture and place sugar side down, lengthways, on the layer of cream. Repeat until the cream is covered, if necessary cut some biscuits to shape, leaving a small gap between each one.

Spoon chocolate cream over the biscuits and repeat the biscuit and cream layers twice more until the tin is full. Depending on their size you may have a few sponge fingers over. Place the cake tin in the freezer, preferably overnight, until the cream is set hard.

To unmould the cake, wrap the loaf tin in a hot damp cloth and invert it onto a flat dish or board tapping the base of the tin to free it. Peel off the food film and discard. Press the toasted almonds into the sides of the cake and replace in the freezer until frozen hard. Cut into slices and serve straight away or wrap in baking paper and food film and store in the freezer until needed.

Boiled Fruit Cake

After discussing war-time cooking - when most baking ingredients were rationed - on a radio programme, I received this recipe for an economical yet excellent fruit cake from a listener in Taunton. The dried fruit is simmered in a mixture of butter, sugar and water before adding the other ingredients and this keeps the cake moist and develops the flavour.

Oven: 160°C/Fan 140°C/Gas 3 **Baking time:** 60-75 minutes **Makes:** 14-21 portions
Equipment: 18 cm (7in.) round or square cake tin - lined

120g (4oz) butter
120g (4oz) demerara sugar
150ml (5fl oz) water
90g (3oz) dried apricots, chopped
90g (3oz) dried dates, chopped
90g (3oz) seedless raisins
90g (3oz) sultanas
90g (3oz) currants
230g (8oz) self-raising flour
½ teaspoon mixed spice
1 large egg, beaten
1-2 tablespoons sherry or orange juice

Measure the butter, sugar and water into a large pan. Add the dried fruit and bring the mixture to the boil. Lower the heat and simmer the mixture gently for 20 minutes. Remove from the heat and stand the pan in cold water until the mixture thickens but is still soft. Add the flour sieved with the spice and mix in the egg and sherry or orange juice.

Turn the mixture into the prepared tin and smooth level. Bake in the preheated oven until a slim bamboo skewer comes out clean from the centre.

Bath Teashop Brownies

Bath has an abundance of charming tea shops where it is all too tempting to linger while sampling their delights. In one of them, I discovered some excellent American-style brownies which are made with plain chocolate, brown sugar and pecan nuts.

Oven: 180°C/Fan 160°C/Gas 4 **Baking time:** 20 minutes **Makes:** 20-25 brownies
Equipment: 20cm (8in.) square cake tin, base-lined

200g (7oz) dessert 50% chocolate
150g (5oz) butter
2 tablespoons of golden syrup
3 eggs
200g (7oz) pale muscovado sugar
few drops of vanilla essence
90g (3oz) flour
120g (4oz) pecan nut halves, split in half lengthways

Break the chocolate into pieces and melt in a dish or bowl over hot water or in a microwave oven. Stir in the butter, cut into small pieces, and the syrup.

Whisk the eggs and sugar with the vanilla essence in a bowl over simmering water until foamy. Use a balloon whisk to fold in the melted chocolate mixture, the flour sieved with the cocoa, and the pecans. Pour the mixture into the prepared tin.

Bake in the preheated oven until the crust is set but the cake gives a little under the pressure of your finger. Try not to overcook the brownies or they may lose their fudge-like quality. My tip for cutting the brownies cleanly is to cool the baked mixture in the tin, chill it overnight, then cut into squares.

Dorset

The noise of the bus on the high road would gradually fade as my father and I walked slowly down the narrow lane, and under the clear skies we passed the bees working the wild honeysuckle in the hedges. Minutes later, we would open a small gate and walk up the garden path to the thatched cottage of Great Aunt Kate. Smiling and white-haired, she leaned on her stick by the rose-covered doorway, waiting to lead us into the sitting room with its wood fire and table laid for tea. Proudly, centre stage, among the cups and plates, would be a gleaming, golden Lardy Cake. What a joy that sweet rich pastry was to a hungry seven-year-old! That experience left me with a life-long fondness for this characteristic West Country treat.

Lard, the rendered fat from a pig, has been an important ingredient in baking for centuries. At a time when almost every cottage kept a pig, fed on household scraps, to provide fresh and cured meat for the autumn and winter, lard was always to hand; and in towns, lard was invariably on sale at the butcher's shop. These days other fats such as butter and vegetable oils are gradually replacing lard in many recipes, yet a Lardy Cake still requires the real thing. Thankfully lard is still plentiful in Dorset, an area long renowned for the quality of its mild-cured bacon and ham.

A more recent Dorset product to have gained nationwide popularity is the non-traditional, cultivated blueberry which is similar in flavour to the smaller bilberries which have grown wild on the heathlands for aeons. Cultivated blueberries are an attractive fruit for eating raw but are also first-rate when cooked, yielding their deep flavour and wine-red colour in cakes, pastries and puddings. Though grown on a small scale in the 1930s, it was the 1946 gift of Canadian blueberry plants - offered to any grower in Britain - that prompted David Trehane, an azalea nurseryman of Stapehill near Wimborne, to try growing this unfamiliar fruit. Nowadays the fresh food shelves of pretty well every supermarket in Britain attest to the huge popularity of such a splendid horticultural venture.

Another Dorset success story can be found not far from Great Aunt Kate's cottage - Cann Mills, one of the most historic flour mills in Dorset. Built on the bank of the Stukel tributary of the river Stour and recorded in the Domesday Book of 1086, Cann Mills survives as a working flour mill and is now run by Stoate & Sons, whose family has been milling grain since 1832. Five pairs of French burr stones are powered by an ancient waterwheel and a more recent Portuguese windmill to produce a range of flours from wheat, spelt and rye grains, some of which are grown locally.

Our growing appetite for wholemeal bread and artisan loaves - both home-made and from small bakeries - has deservedly boosted demand for Stoate Organic Flour throughout the county and even further afield. A widespread concern for good health allied to a quest for satisfying flavour in food is persuading many home bakers, myself included, to extend their skills beyond bread-making to incorporate recipes for delicious cakes, pastry, biscuits and cookies that feature wholemeal flour as a major ingredient.

Recipes for Dorset

120 Fruit and Nut Buttermilk Bread

122 Wholemeal Fruit Scones

123 Hazelnut, Cranberry and Banana Loaf

124 Cann Mills Hot Cross Buns

126 Lardy Cake

128 Spiced Carrot Cake

130 Caraway Seed Cake

131 Matrimony Cake

132 Elderflower and Almond Meringue Cake

134 Chocolate Fondant Cake with Raspberries and Cream

136 Walnut Shortcake topped with Blueberry Meringue

138 Upside-down Orange Marmalade and Pineapple Cake

140 West Country Syllabub

141 Almond Tuiles with Syllabub

142 Custard Tarts

144 Lemon Pies

145 Lemon Curd

146 Dorset Fluffy Cakes with Orange Flower Water

147 Dorset Apple Cake

148 Apricot Trifle Cake

150 Rosemary and Lavender Shortbread Biscuits

151 Ginger Fairings

152 Dorset Chocolate Truffles

Fruit and Nut Buttermilk Bread

The traditional countryside loaf, also known as dairy or soda bread, made in West Country cottages and farmhouses. The bread does not require yeast and instead takes advantage of home-produced buttermilk - the cloudy liquid produced when churning cream into butter. In the past, a simple loaf of flour, bicarbonate of soda and buttermilk was baked over the fire on a griddle, covered with an upturned saucepan to conserve heat. Since buttermilk is not always easy to find, it may be replaced with a 50/50 mixture of plain yoghurt and cold water, and I add rolled oats with dried fruit and chopped nuts to the dough. Serve the bread warm with plenty of unsalted butter or a pot of clotted cream.

Oven: 220°C/Fan 200°C/Gas 7 **Baking time:** 45 minutes **Makes:** 2 small loaves
Equipment: baking sheet, floured; cake tins or foil for covering the dough

500g (1lb 2oz) plain wholemeal flour
120g (4oz) rolled oats
½ teaspoon salt
2 teaspoon bicarbonate of soda
⅛ teaspoon ground cinnamon or grated nutmeg
120g (4oz) soft dried apricots, sliced
120g (4oz) raisins
60g (2oz) cashew, almonds or hazelnuts, roughly chopped
30g (1oz) pumpkin seeds
300ml (10fl oz) buttermilk or diluted yoghurt
150ml (5fl oz) warm water

Measure the flour and oats into a mixing bowl. Sift in the salt, soda and spice and mix in well. Stir in the apricots, raisins, nuts and seeds with the buttermilk and water and quickly blend together until you have a soft, moist dough. Depending on the dryness of the flour you may need a little extra water. Try not to over mix, soda bread should be made quickly and with a light hand.

Divide the dough in two and shape each piece into a round, slightly flattened loaf about 13cm (5 in.) across. Place the bread on the prepared baking sheet and cut an X across the top of each loaf.

Place an upturned cake tin over each loaf, or make a loose hood with aluminium foil, and bake in the preheated oven for 30 minutes. Remove the covers from the loaves and bake for a further 15 minutes until golden and crusty. The bread is cooked when each loaf sounds hollow when tapped on the base. Cool on a wire rack.

Wholemeal Fruit Scones

Locally grown and milled flour contributes even more flavour to these excellent scones.

Oven: 220°C/Fan 200°C/Gas 7 **Baking time:** 20 minutes **Makes:** 8 scones
Equipment: baking sheet, lightly floured

120g (4oz) self-raising flour
2 teaspoons baking powder
60g (2oz) light muscovado sugar
120g (4oz) wholemeal flour
60g (2oz) butter
100g (3½ oz) mixed dried fruit
milk to mix
1 tablespoon sesame seeds

Sift the self-raising flour, baking powder and sugar into a mixing bowl and stir in the wholemeal flour. Rub in the butter and mix in the dried fruit and sufficient milk to make a soft dough. Shape the dough into a circle 15cm (6 in.) across and use a fish slice to transfer to the prepared baking sheet. Mark the dough into 8 wedges cutting halfway through. Brush the top with milk and sprinkle with sesame seeds.

Bake in the centre of the preheated oven until well-risen and golden-brown. Transfer to a wire rack to cool slightly. Serve warm with butter or clotted cream.

Hazelnut, Cranberry and Banana Loaf

Simple and quickly-made teabreads are closer to a traditional teacake than a yeast-leavened fruit loaf. A plate of sliced and buttered teabread is a familiar feature of West Country tea time.

Oven: 180°C/Fan 160°C/Gas 4 **Baking time:** 50-60 minutes **Makes:** 10-12 slice loaf
Equipment: 500g (1lb) loaf tin, buttered and base-lined

90g (3oz) butter
90g (3oz) light muscovado sugar
1 egg
100g (3½ oz) self-raising wholemeal flour
100g (3½ oz) self-raising white flour
¼ teaspoon ground cinnamon
2 large ripe bananas, peeled and sliced
60g (2oz) dried cranberries
90g (3oz) coarsely chopped toasted hazelnuts

Cream the butter with the sugar until light and fluffy. Beat in the egg and stir in the remaining ingredients. Spoon the mixture into the prepared loaf tin and spread level.

Bake in the preheated oven until the loaf is firm but just starting to shrink from the tin. Cool in the tin for 5 minutes then turn out on to a wire rack.

Cann Mills Hot Cross Buns

The Stoate family have been flour millers since 1832, first in Watchet, then Bristol and now at Cann Mills near Shaftesbury. Their organic flours are first-rate and for many years I've made these Good Friday buns using the brown 81% extraction flour. The cross on top of each bun - an indication that these were once ecclesiastical consecrated cakes - can be marked by piping the flour mixture in the recipe.

Oven: 200°C/Fan 180°C/Gas 6 **Baking time:** 20 minutes **Makes:** 18 buns
Equipment: baking sheets - dusted with flour

680g (1lb 8oz) brown flour, 81% extraction
1½ teaspoons rapid-rise dried yeast
½ teaspoon salt
3 teaspoons mixed spice
90g (3oz) caster sugar
90g (3oz) butter
200ml (7fl oz) milk
200ml (7fl oz) boiling water
1 egg, beaten
120g (4oz) currants
60g (2oz) candied peel, chopped

Piping Paste:
45g (1½ oz) self-raising flour
15g (½ oz) butter
5-6 tablespoons milk

Sugar Glaze:
30g (1oz) caster sugar
2 tablespoons water

Measure the flour, yeast, salt, spice and sugar into a mixing bowl and rub in the butter. Mix the milk with the boiling water and, when at blood heat, stir into the dry ingredients with the egg. Mix well and beat with a wooden spoon until the dough becomes elastic. Sprinkle the currants and candied peel over the top of the dough, cover the bowl with a roomy plastic bag and leave in a warm place for 1 hour or until the dough has doubled in size.

Turn the dough onto a floured surface and knead lightly for 2 minutes. Cut the dough into 18 pieces weighing approximately 90g (3oz) each, and shape them into flattish balls. Place the buns on the prepared baking sheets and leave covered in a warm place until well risen. For the crosses, blend the flour with the butter and mix in enough milk to make a smooth piping consistency. Spoon the mixture into a piping bag fitted with a 5 mm (¼ in.) plain nozzle and pipe crosses on the top of each bun.

Bake in the preheated oven until golden brown. Meanwhile dissolve the sugar in the water. Remove the buns from the oven and brush the tops with the glaze then transfer them to a wire rack.

Lardy Cake

For centuries, a few hens, scratching in the grass, and possibly a pig in a sty were the cottager's primary source of animal protein in large areas of rural England. And so rendered pig fat or lard figures in much traditional country baking, sometimes as a replacement for butter and cream. One of the fine, yeast-risen dough cakes which has survived to modern times is the sweet, sticky Lardy Cake also known as Shaley Cake in some parts of the West Country.

Oven: 200°C/Fan 180°C/Gas 6   **Baking time:** 30 minutes   **Makes:** 12-16 portion cake
Equipment: 20cm (8in.) square shallow tin - greased

350g (12oz) white bread flour
1½ teaspoons rapid-rise dried yeast
150ml (5fl oz) warm water
90g (3oz) pure lard
90g (3oz) caster sugar
90g (3oz) currants
pinch mixed spice (optional)

Glaze:
1 tablespoon milk
1 tablespoon caster sugar

Measure the flour and dried yeast into a mixing bowl and stir in the water to make a soft dough. Turn the dough on to a floured surface, knead for 2 minutes then return the dough to the bowl. Cover the bowl with a roomy plastic bag and leave in a warm place for about 1 hour or until the dough has doubled in size.

Meanwhile blend the lard with the sugar and mix in the currants and spice. Turn the dough on to the floured surface and roll out to an oblong measuring 30 x 15cm (12 x 6 in.) Dot two-thirds of the dough with one third of the lard mixture and fold in three as for puff pastry. Re-roll the dough and repeat the larding and folding twice more. Finally, shape the dough into a 20cm (8in.) square and place in the prepared tin. Leave to rise in a warm place for about 1 hour.

Brush the milk over the top of the cake and sprinkle over the sugar. Make two diagonal cuts across the top of the cake and bake in the preheated oven until golden brown. Cool in the tin for 5 minutes then transfer to a wire rack. Lardy Cake is best served slightly warm.

Spiced Carrot Cake

A very good carrot cake which includes West Country soured cream, from the Guild of Cornmillers recipe book. The cake frosting is optional because when freshly baked, and still warm, the cake is already delicious.

Oven: 160°C/Fan 140°C/Gas 3 **Baking time:** 35-40 minutes **Makes:** 16-20 portion cake
Equipment: 20cm (8in.) square tin

120g (4oz) self-raising wholemeal flour
120g (4oz) self-raising flour
175 g (6oz) light muscovado sugar
1½ teaspoons baking powder
1 teaspoon ground cinnamon
½ teaspoon ground allspice
½ teaspoon grated nutmeg
120g (4oz) butter
150g (5fl oz) soured cream
3 eggs
175g (6oz) carrots, coarsely grated
90g (3oz) sultanas
60g (2oz) chopped cashew nuts

Cream Cheese Frosting:
45g (1½ oz) cream cheese
175g (6oz) icing sugar
1-2 drops vanilla essence or grated zest of ½ lemon

Measure the wholemeal flour into a bowl and stir in the white flour sieved with the sugar, baking powder, cinnamon, allspice and nutmeg. Melt the butter in a small pan. Remove from the heat and mix in the soured cream and beaten eggs. Add to the mixing bowl with the grated carrots, sultanas and chopped nuts, and stir until well mixed. Spoon the mixture into the prepared tin and smooth level.

Bake in the preheated oven until a slim bamboo skewer comes out clean from the centre. Cool in the tin for 3 minutes then transfer to a wire rack.

Make the frosting by beating the cream cheese until smooth. Gradually blend in the sieved icing sugar to make a fairly stiff but spreading consistency, then add vanilla essence or lemon zest to taste. Use a palette knife to spread the frosting over the top of the cake and make a pattern of swirls with the blade. Set the cake aside for 1-2 hours until the frosting has set.

Caraway Seed Cake

In 'The Trumpet Major', Thomas Hardy describes a seed-cake as 'so richly compounded that it opened to the knife like a freckled buttercup'. Seed cake dates back centuries though it is rarely baked these days, yet this cake with that pervading aniseed taste imparted by the seeds still has a dedicated following.

Oven: 180°C/Fan 160°C/Gas 4 **Baking time:** 50-60 minutes **Makes:** 10-12 portion cake
Equipment: 1kg (2lb) loaf tin, buttered and base-lined

175g (6oz) butter
175g (6oz) caster sugar
3 eggs
2-3 teaspoons caraway seeds, according to taste
200g (7oz) flour
1 teaspoon baking powder
30g (1oz) ground almonds
1 tablespoon milk

Cream the butter with the sugar until light and fluffy. Beat in the eggs one at a time then mix in the caraway seeds. Sift the flour with the baking powder and fold into the mixture with the ground almonds and the milk. Spoon the mixture into the prepared tin and smooth level.

Bake in the preheated oven until the cake is springy in the centre and a slim bamboo skewer comes out clean. Cool in the tin for 3 minutes then turn out on to a wire rack.

Matrimony Cake

Not a cake at all but a first-rate apple pie enlivened with spices, sugar and lemon. The recipe dates from 1800, according to Theodora Fitzgibbon, who writes that "Matrimonial oracles are traditional to Dorset and take many forms throughout the year. On Midsummer Eve a girl would put her shoes in the form of a T and say this rhyme:

'Hoping this night my true love to see,
I place my shoes in the form of a T.' "

Oven: 180°C/Fan 160°C/Gas 4 **Baking time:** 30-40 minutes **Makes:** 6-8 portion pie
Equipment: 20cm (8in.) pie or tart tin, buttered

230g (8oz) prepared shortcrust pastry
3 tablespoons bread or cake crumbs
3-4 medium dessert apples, peeled and cored
60g (2oz) light muscovado sugar
60g (2oz) mixed seedless raisins and currants
30g (1oz) candied peel, chopped
½ teaspoon grated nutmeg
½ teaspoon ground ginger
1 lemon
2 tablespoons golden syrup
milk to brush the pastry
a little sugar

Roll out just over half the pastry to line the prepared tart tin and scatter the bread or cake crumbs over the pastry. Slice the apples and arrange in overlapping circles on top. Mix together the sugar, dried fruit, candied peel and spices and scatter over the apples. Cut a slice from the middle of the lemon and place in the centre of the apple slices. Trickle the golden syrup over the filling and pour over the strained lemon juice. Roll out the rest of the pastry and cover the pie pressing the edges well together. Brush the top of pie with milk and sprinkle with the sugar.

Bake in a preheated oven until the pastry is golden-brown. Cool slightly then serve hot with thick West Country cream - or for marital bliss - serve the hot pie with cool brandy butter.

Elderflower and Almond Meringue Cake

May-time with dancing around a ribboned maypole has been celebrated for hundreds of years, as the days lengthen and this fertile, almost magical, month dawns. In May, the flat heads of lacy, cream-coloured elderflower blossom appear whose fragrance is captured in the sparkling drink known in the countryside as Elderflower Champagne. As we return to the unspoiled flavours of English country cooking, elderflower cordial has become popular. I add it to the light, frothy cream that sandwiches the discs of almond meringue in this light summery cake.

Oven: 100°C/Fan 90°C/Gas ¼ **Baking time:** 2½-3 hours **Makes:** 8-10 portion cake
Equipment: 2 baking sheets; 2 sheets baking paper

30g (1oz) flaked almonds
4 egg whites
230g (8oz) caster sugar
30g (1oz) ground almonds
1 tablespoon cornflour

Elderflower Cream:
300ml (10fl oz) West Country double cream
4 tablespoons milk
4 tablespoons caster sugar
1-3 teaspoons elderflower cordial
1 egg white

Draw a pencilled circle 20-23cm (8-9 in.) across - I use a plate - on each sheet of paper. Turn over the paper and check the circles are still visible then fix in place on the baking sheets with a smear of butter under each paper corner.

Spread the flaked almonds on another baking sheet and lightly toast under a hot grill, then set aside. Whisk the egg whites with the sugar in a mixing bowl, placed over a pan of gently simmering water, until a thick meringue is formed. This takes 5-7 minutes using a hand-held electric beater. When the meringue forms firm peaks, remove the bowl from the heat and stand it in shallow cold water. Continue to whisk until mixture is cool. Mix the ground almonds with the cornflour and tip into a sieve, sift a little over the surface of the meringue then fold in with a balloon whisk. Spoon the meringue on to the baking paper, keeping it within the pencilled circles, and spread it level. Sprinkle the flaked almonds on top.

Bake the meringues in the preheated oven exchanging the position of the baking sheets half-way through. When properly baked, the discs of meringue should be firm enough to be lifted gently free of the baking paper using a palette knife. Turn off the heat and allow the meringues to cool completely before removing from the oven. If more convenient, the meringue layers can be stored, in a lidded plastic box, in a freezer until required.

Whisk the cream with the milk until thick but still glossy. Stir in half the the sugar and elderflower cordial to taste. Whisk the egg white until stiff then whisk in the remaining sugar and fold into the cream. Place one disc of meringue on a serving plate, spoon the cream on top and cover with the other meringue. Chill the cake for 1 hour before serving.

Chocolate Fondant Cake with Raspberries and Cream

A real delight for serving at a birthday lunch or tea party. The velvety, dark, fudge-like cake with ground almonds in place of wheat flour is topped with thick cream and ripe raspberries or halved strawberries.

Oven: 160°C/Fan 140°C/Gas 3 **Baking time:** 30-35 minutes **Makes:** 8-10 portion cake
Equipment: 23cm (9 in.) spring-clip tin, base-lined

Cake:
230g (8oz) plain 70% chocolate
175g (6oz) dark muscovado sugar
175g (6oz) butter
60g (2oz) ground almonds
30g (1oz) cocoa powder
4 eggs, separated
¼ teaspoon vanilla essence
1 tablespoon brandy, armagnac or rum

Cream:
300ml (10fl oz) double cream
4 tablespoons whole milk
1 tablespoon caster sugar
few drops vanilla essence
150g (5oz) raspberries or small strawberries

Break the chocolate into pieces in a heatproof mixing bowl and place in the preheated oven or over a pan of simmering water until the chocolate has melted. Stir gently until smooth, then mix in the sugar and butter cut into pieces. Add the ground almonds and cocoa powder with the egg yolks blended with the vanilla essence and brandy and stir until well combined. Whisk the egg whites until stiff and gradually fold into the mixture. Spoon the mixture into the prepared tin and smooth level.

Bake in the preheated oven until a slim bamboo skewer comes out clean from the centre of the cake. Cool the cake in the tin then transfer the cake on its baking paper to a flat serving dish. If you wish the cake can be left, covered loosely with a plastic bag, in a cool place overnight.

Whisk the cream with the milk until thick but still glossy. Mix in the sugar and vanilla essence and spoon over the top of the cake. Arrange the raspberries on the cream and set aside the cake in a cool place for serving the same day.

Walnut Shortcake topped with Blueberry Meringue

Dorset blueberries have been grown by the Trehane family in Wimborne for almost seventy years and, at last, this midnight-blue fruit has become hugely popular. Blueberries are one of the best newcomers to the cornucopia of West Country foods - high in vitamin content and with a distinctive flavour. This cake has an appealing combination of nuts and fresh fruit - replace blueberries with raspberries, if you prefer - and tastes at its best while still warm or within a few hours of baking.

Oven: 180°C/Fan 160°C/Gas 4 then 150°C/Fan 130°C/Gas 2 **Baking time:** 35-40 minutes
Makes: 16 squares **Equipment:** 23cm (9in.) square shallow tin, buttered and base-lined

Walnut Shortcake:
100g (3½ oz) walnut pieces
150g (5oz) self-raising flour
60g (2oz) butter
100g (3½ oz) light muscovado sugar
2 egg yolks
few drops of vanilla essence
150ml (5fl oz) milk

Meringue Layer:
2 egg whites
100g (3½ oz) caster sugar
300g (10oz) blueberries or raspberries
1 tablespoon granulated sugar

Reserve 1 tablespoon of walnut pieces for the top of the cake and tip the remainder into the bowl of a food processor with the flour. Process for a few seconds until the nuts are coarsely chopped. Cream the butter with the sugar, egg yolks and vanilla essence and stir in the flour/nut blend and milk alternately to make a soft mixture. Spoon the mixture into the prepared tin and spread level.

Bake in the preheated oven for 20 minutes or until a slim wooden skewer comes out clean from the centre of the cake.

Remove the cake from the oven and prepare the meringue. Whisk the egg whites until stiff and gradually whisk in the sugar. Fold in the fruit and spread the meringue over the warm cake. Roughly chop the reserved walnuts and sprinkle them with the granulated sugar over the top of the meringue.

Bake the cake for a further 15-20 minutes or until the meringue is slightly golden. Cool the cake in the tin for 15 minutes then cut into portions and serve.

WEST COUNTRY CAKES & ASSORTED FANCIES

Upside-down Orange Marmalade and Pineapple Cake

On a brisk walk in deepest winter along the Dorset coastal path, the vision of a hot marmalade cake waiting at home promptly speeds one's steps. Serve the cake with the hot fruit sauce and scoops of vanilla ice cream.

Oven: 180°C/Fan 160°C/Gas 4 **Baking time:** 60-70 minutes **Makes:** 9 portion cake
Equipment: 23cm (9 in.) square cake tin, lined

Fruit Layer:
3 medium-size sweet oranges, Navel or seedless
30g (1oz) butter
60g (2oz) light muscovado sugar
230g (8oz) tin pineapple rings in juice

Cake:
175g (6oz) butter
175g (6oz) light muscovado sugar
2 eggs
3 heaped tablespoons orange marmalade
175g (6oz) self-raising wholemeal flour
175g (6oz) self-raising flour
¼ teaspoon grated nutmeg
3-4 tablespoons pineapple juice, from the tin

Sauce:
1 teaspoon cornflour blended with 1 tablespoon water
sugar to taste

Wash and dry the oranges. Cut 9 fairly thin slices from two of the fruit and squeeze the juice from the ends of the fruit into a teacup and set aside. Cook the orange slices with 4 tablespoons water in a covered pan for 10 minutes over moderate heat or until the peel is soft. Drain the orange slices on kitchen paper and add the cooking liquid to the cup.

Melt the butter in a small pan. Remove from the heat, cool slightly then stir in the sugar and pour the butter/sugar mixture into the base of the prepared cake tin. Arrange the 9 orange slices on top - 3 by 3 - and place pieces of drained pineapple rings in the gaps. Puree the remaining pineapple with its juice in a processor then pour into the small buttery pan with the orange juice from the teacup.

Cream the butter with the sugar until light and fluffy. Beat in the eggs separately. Mix in the marmalade and both types of flour with the nutmeg and finely grated zest of half of the third orange. Spoon the mixture into the cake tin, taking care to keep the fruit in place, smooth level.

Bake in the preheated oven until the cake is cooked and a slim bamboo skewer comes out clean from the centre. Leave the cake in the tin while you prepare the sauce.

To the small pan, add the finely grated zest and juice of the remaining half of the third orange. Blend the cornflour and water and add to the pan, then cook the mixture stirring until thickened. If necessary, sweeten with sugar and pour into a small jug. Turn out the cake, fruit side on top onto a flat board or plate and cut into 9 portions. Serve with the hot sauce and spoonfuls of thick cream or ice cream.

West Country Syllabub

A delicate concoction of cream and alcohol, described by the food historian, Ivan Day, as 'surely the most Arcadian of all English summer refreshments'. Recipes for syllabub, dating from the seventeenth century, mainly agree on the ingredients: sweetened and spiced cider or wine, sometimes fortified with brandy or sherry, and thick cream whisked together until frothy. If left to stand, the syllabub may separate with the cream on top - eaten with a spoon - and the alcohol below - which is sipped. In an early recipe, extra lightness in a syllabub is provided by stiffly-whisked egg white while in 1784, Elizabeth Raffald, adds lemon juice to her mixture.
This syllabub is made with thick cream, lemon juice, a splash of cider or
perry with brandy, and the traditional garnish of sprigs of fresh rosemary.

Serves: 4-6
1 large lemon
100ml (3½fl oz) cider or perry and 2 tablespoons brandy
pinch of grated nutmeg
60g (2oz) caster sugar
300ml (10fl oz) double cream
1 egg white and 1 tablespoon caster sugar (optional)
4-6 sprigs of fresh rosemary

Use a lemon zester to remove some fine threads of peel from the lemon for
decorating the syllabub and set aside. Trim a strip of peel from the lemon and place in a bowl with the strained juice from the lemon. Add the cider, brandy, nutmeg and sugar and stir until dissolved. Cover the bowl and set aside for 1 hour or longer.

Discard the strip of lemon peel and pour 1 tablespoon of the mixture into each of 4-6 medium size wine glasses. Whisk the cream until thick but still glossy and gradually whisk in the rest of the lemon/cider mixture taking care not to whisk the mixture for too long.

If you wish to lighten the syllabub, whisk the egg white until stiff and whisk in the tablespoon of caster sugar. Gently fold this into the cream mixture. Carefully spoon the syllabub into each glass and sprinkle a few strands of lemon zest and garnish with the sprigs of rosemary.
Serve straight away or within an hour while the mixture is still frothy.

Almond Tuiles with Syllabub

Crisp, almond biscuits curved like Provencal tiles to accompany a delicate West Country Syllabub made with cider or perry and brandy.

Oven: 190°C/Fan 170°C/Gas 5 **Baking time:** 7-8 minutes **Makes:** 24 - 30 biscuits
Equipment: baking sheet, lined; wooden rolling pin for shaping the biscuits

60g (2oz) butter
2 egg whites
120g (4oz) caster sugar
60g (2oz) flour
60g (2oz) flaked almonds

Melt the butter in a pan and set aside in a warm place. Whisk the egg whites until foamy but not dry. Add half the sugar and whisk in again, repeat with the rest of the sugar. Fold in the sieved flour and the melted butter with the almonds. Place teaspoonfuls of the mixture on the prepared baking sheet, allowing plenty of room for the biscuits to spread. Make the biscuits in batches unless you have several rolling pins for shaping them.

Bake in the preheated oven until golden. Use a palette knife to remove each biscuit and immediately place on the rolling pin so that it takes up the curved shape. Remove the biscuits as soon as they have cooled and store in an air-tight container.

Custard Tarts

West Country cream makes these classic tarts particularly rich and delectable. The filling is adapted from Hannah Glasse's baked custard in *The Art of Cookery made Plain and Easy* (1747). The custard is a simple but lovely blend of eggs and cream flecked with nutmeg and cinnamon and scented with rose-petal and orange flower water.

Oven: 200°C/Fan 180°C/Gas 6 then 180°C/160°C/Gas 4 **Baking time:** 25-30 minutes **Makes:** about 12 tarts **Equipment:** 7.5cm (3in.) pastry cutter, deep patty or small muffin tins, buttered

Rich Shortcrust Pastry:
120g (4oz) flour
30g (1oz) caster sugar
60g (2oz) butter, softened
1 egg yolk

Custard:
300ml (10fl oz) single cream
30g (1oz) caster sugar
2 eggs
pinch of freshly grated nutmeg
pinch of ground cinnamon
pinch of ground mace
rosewater and orange flower water

Sieve the flour and sugar into a bowl. Add the butter and egg yolk and work together with the fingertips to make a soft dough. Chill the dough and the prepared patty tins in a fridge for 15 minutes. On a lightly floured board, roll out the pastry dough thinly and cut out circles with the pastry cutter. Line the prepared patty tins with the pastry circles and prick the base of each tart with a fork to let out the air while baking. Place the lined patty tins back in the fridge for 15 minutes until well chilled.

Bake the pastry cases in the preheated oven at the higher temperature for 10-12 minutes until the pastry is just changing colour. Remove from the oven and reduce the heat to the lower temperature.

Make the custard by whisking the cream with the sugar and the eggs and strain into a jug. Stir in the spices and add the flower waters to taste. Carefully pour or spoon the custard into the pastry cases and replace in the oven for 15-20 minutes until the custard is just set. Cool the tarts in the patty tins then carefully transfer to a wire rack. Serve the tarts while still warm or not quite cold.

Lemon Pies

Delectable tartlets, based on an old recipe for little lemon pies made with clotted cream.

Oven: 200°C/Fan 180°C/Gas 6 **Baking time:** 12-15 minutes **Makes:** 12 tarts
Equipment: 7.5 cm (3 in.) fluted pastry cutter, patty tins - buttered

Pastry:
120g (4oz) flour
15g (½ oz) caster sugar
60g (2oz) butter, softened
1 egg, beaten

Filling:
lemon curd
clotted cream
few strands of lemon zest

Sieve the flour and sugar into a shallow mixing bowl or on to a cold work surface. Add the butter and half the beaten egg and use the fingertips to mix the ingredients together. Slide small handfuls of the mixture sideways until the dough easily forms a ball, adding a little extra egg if the mixture is too dry to cohere. Wrap the pastry in plastic and chill for 15 minutes.

Roll out the pastry thinly on a lightly floured surface and use the cutter to make 12 circles - usually I cut 8 first and re-roll the trimmings for the other 4. Line the patty tins with the pastry circles, gently pressing them into place. Lightly prick the bases and chill the patty tin for 15 minutes.

Bake the pastry cases blind in the preheated oven until the pastry is cooked with the edges pale brown. Place the tray on a heatproof work surface and turn off the oven. Place a rounded teaspoons of lemon curd in each pastry case and spoon clotted cream on top. Replace the patty tray in the oven and leave for a few minutes for the curd and cream to run together until level. Remove from the oven and sprinkle a few strands of lemon zest on each tartlet. Allow the tarts to cool completely before carefully lifting them onto a serving plate.

Lemon Curd

Home-made fruit curds are one of Britain's most traditional preserves. The flavour of lemon curd is at its best when freshly-made and so I prefer to prepare a small amount at a time and store the jars in the refrigerator. When making lemon curd, use a china or heatproof glass bowl and a wooden or plastic spoon - metal implements can impair the taste.

2 lemons, ideally organic and unwaxed
120g (4oz) caster sugar
2 eggs
120g (4oz) unsalted butter

Wash and dry the lemons. Grate the lemon zest into a bowl placed over a pan of gently simmering water. Add the strained juice, sugar and eggs. Cook, stirring all the time, for 10-15 minutes until the mixture is thick enough to coat the back of a spoon. Remove the bowl from the heat and gradually beat in the butter, adding it in small pieces. Spoon the curd into a small dish or jar. Cover with food film and store in the refrigerator until needed.

Dorset Fluffy Cakes with Orange Flower Water

Snowy-white, small cakes scented with orange flower water and shreds of orange zest, these cakes are also wheat-free.

Oven: 180°C/Fan 160°C/Gas 4 **Baking time:** 12-15 minutes **Makes:** 18-20 cakes
Equipment: two 12-cup patty tins, lined with paper cases

120g (4oz) caster sugar
2 eggs
1 teaspoon orange flower water
1 orange
230g (8oz) cornflour
1 teaspoon baking powder
120g (4oz) icing sugar

Soften the butter in a bowl and beat in the sugar until pale and fluffy. Beat the eggs with ½ teaspoon of orange flower water and the finely grated zest and juice of half the orange and add to the bowl alternately with the cornflour and baking powder, mixing well each time. Place rounded dessertspoons of the mixture in the paper cases.

Bake in the preheated oven until the cakes are well risen and golden brown. Cool the cakes in the patty tins.

Mix the icing sugar with ½ teaspoon of orange flower water and 3-4 teaspoons orange juice to make a spreadable glace icing. Use a teaspoon to trickle icing over each cake and sprinkle a few strands of orange zest on top. Leave the cakes in a warm place until the icing is set.

Dorset Apple Cake

The recipe for this simple yet excellent apple cake comes from Maiden Newton. Serve the cake warm, as it is or accompanied by clotted cream or thick plain yoghurt. Alternative versions made with summer fruits such as ripe gooseberries, raspberries or halved strawberries are also recommended.

Oven: 180°C/Fan 160°C/Gas 4 **Baking time:** 40-45 minutes **Makes:** 8-10 portions
Equipment: 20cm (8 in.) sponge cake tin, buttered

3-4 medium size eating apples
1 small lemon
350 g (8oz) self-raising flour
120g (4oz) caster sugar
120g (4oz) butter
1 egg
3-4 tablespoons milk

Peel, core and quarter the apples and cut across into slices. Weigh 230g (8 oz) of the apple slices and tip them into a small bowl and stir in the finely grated zest and juice of the lemon. Measure the flour and sugar into a mixing bowl, add the butter in small pieces and rub into the mixture with the fingertips. Stir in the apples with the beaten egg and add milk to make a stiff mixture. Spoon into the prepared cake tin and spread level.

Bake in the preheated oven until golden-brown. Cool the cake in the tin for 10 minutes then transfer to a serving plate or wooden board and cut into portions.

Apricot Trifle Cake

Apricot trees are sometimes to be found in sheltered West Country gardens. Once established, they often produce a good crop of their velvety, flame-coloured fruit. Small or late-season apricots are ideal for this trifle-like cake which is not baked, just assembled. If preferred, a puree of poached pears or apples can replace the apricots. Layers of sponge fingers are dipped in fruit brandy and sandwiched with apricot puree and chopped dried fruit and almonds then topped with whipped cream. A rich yet simple cake that is best made a day ahead and chilled in a fridge until ready to serve.

Equipment: 20cm (8in.) square cake tin, lined **Makes:** 12-16 portion cake

500g (1lb 2oz) fresh apricots
230g (8oz) caster sugar
150ml (5fl oz) water
100g (3½ oz) seedless raisins or sultanas
100g (3½ oz) ready-to-eat prunes, chopped
60g (2oz) stem ginger, in syrup or crystallised, chopped
45g (1½ oz) flaked almonds, toasted
8 tablespoons apricot brandy or liqueur
about 50 sponge fingers
2 leaves or 1 tablespoon powdered gelatine
300ml (10fl oz) whipping or double cream

Halve then quarter the apricots, discarding the stones. Dissolve the sugar in the water in a pan over moderate heat, add the apricots and cook until tender. Cool slightly then pour the liquid from the fruit into a measuring jug and puree the apricots in blender or processor until smooth.

Measure the raisins, prunes, ginger and ⅔ of the flaked almonds into a bowl and stir in half the apricot brandy.

Pour the rest of the brandy into a shallow dish and add half the apricot liquid. Briefly dip the non-sugared side of a sponge finger into the liquid and place, sugar side down, in the base of the prepared cake tin. Repeat until the base is covered with 14-16 biscuits, arranged side by side in two neat rows, filling in any gaps with small pieces.

Scatter half the dried fruit mixture on top and spoon over half the apricot puree in an even layer. Repeat the layer of dipped biscuits, arranging them in the same way, and spoon on the rest of the dried fruit and puree. Place the final layer of dipped biscuits sugar side up and cover with a sheet of baking paper. Place a board over the cake tin and chill the cake in the refrigerator overnight. Cover and chill the remaining apricot liquid.

Next day, remove the covering paper and carefully unmould the cake on a flat serving plate and gently peel off the baking paper. In a small pan over low heat, soften the gelatine in the reserved apricot liquid, stirring until dissolved. Cool by standing the pan in shallow cold water but remove before the gelatine sets.

Whisk the cream until stiff but still glossy, carry on slowly whisking while you pour in the apricot mixture in a steady trickle. Spoon the cream over the cake, and scatter the remaining toasted almonds over the top. Replace the cake in the refrigerator to set.

When ready to serve, use a long sharp knife to mark out 16 portions, then cut through and use a palette knife to transfer each piece to a small plate for serving.

Rosemary and Lavender Shortbread Biscuits

A few, finely-chopped leaves of rosemary or lavender give these shortbread biscuits a lovely fragrance and flavour.

Oven: 160°C/Fan 140°C/Gas 3 **Baking time:** 15-17 minutes **Makes:** about 20 biscuits
Equipment: 6cm (2½ in.) fluted pastry cutter, baking sheet, buttered

120g (4oz) butter
½ teaspoon finely chopped leaves of rosemary or lavender
60g (2oz) caster sugar
175g (6oz) flour
1 tablespoon caster sugar

In a warmed mixing bowl, beat the butter with the chopped leaves until soft. Add the sugar and cream together. Gradually add the sieved flour and continue beating until the mixture binds together in a lump. On a floured board, roll out the dough until 0.5cm (¼ in.) thick. Use the pastry cutter to cut out rounds of dough. Place on the prepared baking sheet and prick each biscuit a couple of times with a fork.

Bake in the preheated oven until just changing colour at the edges. Do not overcook or the subtle buttery flavour will be lost. Cool on the baking sheet for 3 minutes then transfer to a wire rack and sprinkle with the extra caster sugar.

Ginger Fairings

A traditional, crisp biscuit once sold at country fairs throughout the year. Ginger fairings play a small part in the plot of Thomas Hardy's 'Jude the Obscure'.

Oven: 190°C/Fan 170°C/Gas 5 **Baking time:** 10-12 minutes **Makes:** 30 biscuits
Equipment: non-stick baking sheet

120g (4oz) butter
30g (1oz) golden syrup
90g (3oz) light soft brown sugar
175g (6oz) flour
1 teaspoon ground ginger
½ teaspoon bicarbonate of soda

Measure the butter and syrup into a pan and melt over low heat. Remove from the heat and stir in the sugar. Add the flour sieved with the ginger and bicarbonate of soda and mix until well combined. Take teaspoons of the mixture and roll into balls, then flatten them onto the baking sheet.

Bake in the preheated oven until golden. Cool on the baking sheet for 2-3 minutes then transfer to a wire rack.

Dorset Chocolate Truffles

These tempting chocolate truffles are simple to make, they contain thick West Country cream and are flavoured with tangerine or cognac.

Makes: about 75 truffles

200g (7oz) plain 70% chocolate
300ml (10fl oz) double cream
1 tangerine, finely grated zest and strained juice
1-2 tablespoons cognac or armagnac
caster sugar
dark cocoa powder
small paper cases

Break the chocolate into very small pieces in a mixing bowl. Heat the cream until it it almost boiling and immediately pour it over the chocolate. Stir until the chocolate has melted. If you wish to flavour the truffles, mix in the zest and juice of the tangerine or the cognac or even both. But omit these if you prefer the chocolate to taste of itself. Taste the mixture, you may wish to sweeten the mixture a little by stirring in some sugar. Stand the bowl in shallow, cold water to cool the mixture then leave in a cool place or refrigerate it until the mixture is thick enough to spoon into shape.

Line a tray or some baking sheets with baking paper. Use a teaspoon to scoop bite-size portions and place them on the paper and chill for 30 minutes.

To finish the truffles make a layer of cocoa in a shallow dish and use two forks to pick up each truffle. Dip and roll it in the cocoa, if need be press into the sides of the truffle with the prongs of the fork so that it resembles a little log. Transfer each finished truffle to serving dish, or place each one in a small paper case. Keep the truffles chilled until ready to serve.

NOTES

NOTES

NOTES

NOTES

Acknowledgements

First and foremost, my gratitude goes to my daughter-in-law, Sarah Rauchas, for her warm recommendation to the publisher, Ron Johns, who invited me to write this book. Debbie Watson has been an admirable editor - kind, understanding and conscientious. It has been a joy to work with Rebecca Cobb whose delightful illustrations adorn the book. My thanks also go to my many friends in the West Country who have provided recipes, anecdotes and memories that have made researching this book such a pleasure.

Also by Geraldene Holt

GERALDENE HOLT'S CAKE STALL
TRAVELLING FOOD
BUDGET GOURMET
TUCK BOX TREATS
FRENCH COUNTRY KITCHEN
RECIPES FROM A FRENCH HERB GARDEN
THE GOURMET GARDEN
A CUP OF TEA
THE COOK'S ROOM (contributor)
COMPLETE BOOK OF HERBS
COUNTRY HOUSE COOKING
DIARY OF A FRENCH HERB GARDEN
GERALDENE HOLT'S CAKES